MORALITY: RELIGIOUS AND SECULAR

MORALITY: RELIGIOUS AND SECULAR

The Dilemma of the Traditional Conscience

BY

BASIL MITCHELL

Nolloth Professor of the Philosophy of the Christian Religion in the University of Oxford

CLARENDON PRESS · OXFORD
1980

Oxford University Press, Walton Street, Oxford OX2 6DP

OXFORD LONDON GLASGOW
NEW YORK TORONTO MELBOURNE WELLINGTON
KUALA LUMPUR SINGAPORE JAKARTA HONG KONG TOKYO
DELHI BOMBAY CALCUTTA MADRAS KARACHI
NAIROBI DAR ES SALAAM CAPE TOWN

Published in the United States
by Oxford University Press, New York

British Library Cataloguing in Publication Data

Mitchell, Basil
Morality.
1. Ethics
I. Title
170 BJ1012 79-42792

ISBN 0-19-824537-8

Set in IBM Baskerville by Graphic Services, Oxford
Printed in Great Britain by
Lowe and Brydone,
Thetford

To M. E. M.

Preface

This book is a somewhat revised version of the Gifford Lectures delivered at the University of Glasgow in 1974 and 1975. Lord Gifford wished the lectures given on his foundation to be 'popular', by which I take him to have meant 'non-technical'. I have tried to comply with his wish, not only because he expressed it, but for two further reasons. The first is that the subject is of interest and concern to the general reader. The second is that it is no longer possible for a single individual to master all the disciplines that are required for a full academic treatment of it. He would need to be a philosopher, a theologian, a sociologist, and a historian at the very least. Yet it remains necessary to attempt something on a fairly large scale because important issues otherwise go by default. If philosophers always confine themselves to small-scale manageable problems of the sort that can be handled with full analytical rigour they are exposed, by their very concentration, to the risk of allowing fundamental assumptions to go uncriticized and even, perhaps, unnoticed. It looks as if the only practicable solution is a sketch large enough in scale to reveal these wider assumptions, but with enough detail to display the argument clearly and enable it to be checked. The whole will be too obviously incomplete to masquerade as a finished picture.

Such a compromise is beset with difficulties, and I am, therefore, more than usually aware of the many debts that I owe. First I must thank the University of Glasgow for the invitation to deliver the lectures and for the overwhelmingly generous hospitality which my wife and I received during our visits in two successive years. I am grateful to Colgate University, New York, and the University of Canterbury, New Zealand for the opportunity to give some of the lectures again, and for the stimulus provided by, in particular, Professor R. V. Smith of Colgate and Mr J. C. Thornton of Canterbury. I have received continuous help and encouragement from Mr J. R. Lucas. Those who, at various stages, have read the manuscript in whole or in part and have helped me with their comments, are too numerous for me to mention all of them. They include Professor John Howes, Professor Gene Outka, Professor C. R. Kordig, Dr R. J. Delahunty, and Dr Eleanor Dand.

In addition I owe a special debt to Professor R. M. Hare. His contributions to moral philosophy have been so influential that it would have been impossible in a study like this either to ignore them or to do them justice, let alone to match their clarity and rigour. In philosophy there is no greater compliment than dissent, and I am grateful for the stimulus and challenge of his thought over many years.

Contents

I

Introduction: Our Contemporary Moral Confusion

In this book I want to consider the relationship between morality and religion—whether morality needs a religious sanction; and what difference, if any, religious belief makes to the scope, character, and content of morality. Most people would feel bound to agree that these are important questions, but many, if they are honest, would admit to finding them rather boring. And this for two reasons: they take the answers to be obvious; and they find the questions lacking in any immediate contemporary relevance.

As to obviousness, it is quite true that, if you ask people whether religion makes any difference to morality, they will generally regard the answer as obvious. But it soon becomes apparent that some take the answer to be obviously 'yes' and others take it to be equally obviously 'no'. The question, once raised, turns out to be highly controversial, although comparatively little controversy actually takes place. This absence of actual controversy is due partly to the fact that intellectuals as a class (including professional philosophers) have for some time taken the total independence of morality from religion for granted, while those who think otherwise are not, as a rule, intellectuals. When they are heard at all, they are not taken seriously. But it is also due in part to the belief that there still exists a broad working consensus in ethics which makes it unnecessary, and even unwise, to raise fundamental issues of justification. No doubt past ages were never as homogeneous as they seem in retrospect, but until comparatively recently people could to some extent take for granted a continuous ethical tradition which, although it had been challenged, still enjoyed general acceptance.

We, however, can no longer do so, for that tradition is now visibly disintegrating. Nothing is more striking than our present confusion and perplexity about morality. We find ourselves in the situation in which, with Socrates and Plato, moral philosophy first came into existence. When the customary foundations of morality are sufficiently shaken, there is no alternative but to examine them carefully and then replace or restore them. It is for this reason that, of all moral philosophers, Plato speaks most directly to our present condition. *The Republic,* with its classical statement of the problem of the justification of morality has, within a generation, ceased to be a historical monument and become a work of disconcerting relevance. It is critics of Plato, such as H. A. Prichard, for whom the problem could not arise because moral duties are self-evident, who now appear as historical curiosities. In such a confused situation the questions that I propose to ask cannot be presumed to be irrelevant, nor the answers to them obvious.

Let me first illustrate what I have in mind in speaking of perplexity and confusion. Imagine an article in *The Times* deploring a decline in moral standards, and instancing the continuing rise in convictions for crimes of violence, the greater incidence of divorce and abortion, the prevalence of pornography, the growth of corruption in public life; and then imagine the character of the ensuing correspondence. There would, no doubt, be some dispute about the facts. What date is taken as the base for the comparison? Were statistics at that time compiled on the same principles or with the same degree of thoroughness as they are today? But, suppose the statistical facts to be agreed, do they represent a moral decline? We need to know, some will say, why it is that people are less prepared to refrain from the activities complained of than they used to be. To the extent that the answer is that they refrained in the past out of fear of punishment, or social condemnation, or economic insecurity, or even from unthinking acquiescence in customary attitudes, then, these people will say, there was no moral value in their restraint. In our more permissive age *genuine* morality is perhaps no rarer, and may even be more prevalent, than it was when other forms of social control could be relied upon with greater confidence. It will also be argued by some, and perhaps the same people, that in any case not all of these changes in behaviour *are* to be deplored. A distinction should be made, for example, between divorce, abortion, and pornography on the one hand and violence and corruption on the other. Questions of sexual behaviour are essentially personal and it is for individuals alone to decide what is right and wrong in these matters. A social situation which permits greater freedom of choice in this area is greatly to be welcomed. But to injure or cheat others is to offend against a public morality which we all have an interest in maintaining. Even this proposition will not, however, win general acceptance. It depends, some will say, on the credentials of the system which our public morality is being used to safeguard. If it is unjust, in that it denies satisfaction to particular individuals or classes, then these individuals or classes are under no obligation to embrace its morality. The incidence of violent crime. if not of corruption, should be seen as a natural and justifiable revolt of the relatively deprived against those who have, intentionally or unintentionally, connived at their deprivation. Yet others will be found to champion violence in itself as an authentic expression of the human spirit because it alone is able to avoid the compromises which infect all constructive effort and so attains an absolute purity of motive. Two other voices at least are likely to be raised in our imagined correspondence; one is that of those who maintain that the entire dispute is vitiated by a failure to recognize the inevitable relativity of moral claims. There has been no decline in morals because the very conception of such a decline is incoherent, since moral attitudes are either irredeemably subjective or relative to particular cultures or subcultures; and the other is that of those who insist that we are in no position to tell whether what we are experiencing constitutes a decline in morality, because the necessary scientific research which alone could provide us with an appropriate morality for our time has not yet been undertaken.

The careful reader of these imagined letters could not fail to notice the extent to which their writers are divided not only in their opinions but in their vocabulary. They inhabit different worlds of discourse, and are perpetually arguing at cross purposes—when, that is, they bother to argue at all. More often they are content to address themselves exclusively to those who share their convictions, using for the purpose the editorial 'we' in such a way as (quite literally) to excommunicate any who might disagree with them. Thus Lionel

Trilling in *Sincerity and Authenticity* quotes George Eliot's famous conversation with F. W. H. Myers while walking in the Fellows' Garden of Trinity College, Cambridge in which she referred to God as inconceivable, to immortality as unbelievable, but to duty as 'peremptory and absolute' and comments:

> We of our time do not share that need of the Victorians. We are not under the necessity of discovering in the order of the universe, in the ineluctable duty it silently lays upon us, the validation of such personal coherence and purposiveness as we claim for ourselves. We do not ask those questions which would suggest that the validation is indeed there, needing only to be discovered; to us they seem merely factitious.[1]

It is plain that not all of us are 'we'.

It is not surprising that in this confused situation there is a common reluctance to use explicitly moral language or to carry a moral argument through to a conclusion, although even this generalization needs to be qualified. There may coexist, often in the same individuals, a wary scouting of moral vocabulary (or what has customarily passed for such) and an intensity of protest against prevailing attitudes and practices which has all the marks of deep moral indignation. It is as if the specifically moral impulse, denied its traditional outlets, has poured with enormous pressure into the few remaining channels that the fashion of the day allows. John Searle, in his study of the radical student movement in America in the 1960s,[2] notices the importance of such 'sacred topics' as race and the Vietnam War. To arouse support a challenge to the university's authority had to relate some local issue to a 'sacred topic'.

Two instances must suffice of the suspicion or repudiation of moral language. Stephen Jessel writing in *The Times*[3] attributed a new philosophy to the young: 'Its practitioners refuse to acknowledge the principle of moral responsibility for others; they decline to talk of the actions of other people in moral phraseology. When pressed they often reduce their own set of values to a simple pleasure-pain antithesis.' Also in an article in *The Times*[4] the playwright Dennis Potter asked why the television script writer should bother to challenge official

[1] Oxford University Press (1972), p. 118.
[2] *The Campus War*, Penguin (1972).
[3] *The Times*, 14 Aug. 1967.
[4] *The Times*, 5 July 1969.

complacency in the discharge of his ephemeral task: 'I hesitate to use the word "Duty" because it has, mysteriously, coated itself with increasingly weird connotations.' In a perceptive review of this phenomenon[5] Malcolm Bradbury quoted an early example from Richard Aldington's *Farewell to Arms*: 'There were many words you could not stand to hear and finally only the names of places had dignity . . . Abstract words such as glory, honour, courage, or hallow were obscene.' The use of the word 'obscene' in this way, now common, represents an interesting development in itself.

As to systematic changes in vocabulary, here are two illustrations from the field of education. A note in the Schools Bulletin published by the West Riding County Council Education Committee[6] called attention to the words which for the moment were 'out' and to others that were 'in' within the world of education. There followed two lists, of which I give a selection:

'Out' words	*'In' words*
Duty	Anti-social
Evil	Uncooperative
Bad	Open-ended
Wicked	Creative
Scholar	Integrated
Naughty	Participation
Studious	Meaningful
Clever	Awareness
Subject	Relationships
Method	Involvement
Punishment	Treatment
Standards	On-going
Dull	Under achieving

A noticeable feature of the second list is the absence of explicitly moral words of praise or blame, although approval or disapproval is more or less clearly implied. 'Open-ended' and 'on-going' are obviously 'pro' words; 'anti-social' and 'uncooperative' 'con' words.

In a letter to *The Times*[7] Mr Gareth Rees rebutted criticism

[5] 'The New Language of Morals' in *Twentieth Century*, Summer 1963.
[6] January 1970.
[7] *The Times*, 25 July 1974.

of trends in comprehensive schools and defended the school in which he taught: 'I believe there is as much, probably more, old-fashioned good Christianity in this egalitarian, atheistic, progressive, trendy, hard-swearing, free-loving comprehensive than in any religious, excellent, patriotic, single-sex, single caste establishment.' This is a particularly complex example since Mr Rees not only uses his own pro-words to express approval: 'egalitarian, progressive', and his opponents' pro-words to express disapproval: 'religious, excellent, patriotic'; but also his opponents' con-words to express approval: 'trendy, hard-swearing, free-loving'; *and* his opponents' pro-words to express approval: 'old-fashioned, good Christianity'. I cannot forbear adding a recent American example—this time from outside the field of education. On Saturday 11 September 1976 the *New York Times* carried a report on the problems of Woodstock N.Y. caused by the influx of young people since the Woodstock Rock Festival of seven years ago: 'The townspeople call the young people hippies, freaks, longhairs, countercultures or just "those people". "I don't call them hippies" said Chief Constable William Waterous. "I call them drifters and bums because that's what they are."'

Underlying this linguistic confusion one can, I think, discern disagreement on three basic questions. There are differences as to what is right or wrong, good or bad; and hence as to what moral concepts to employ. There are differences as to whether there is such a thing as morality. And there are differences as to what, if morality does exist, is the point or purpose of it. Disagreements as to what is right or wrong, good or bad are often not settled, or even made explicit enough to be discussed, because of disagreements on the other questions. To clarify these questions and the relations between them is pre-eminently a task for philosophers, but philosophers themselves are involved in the cultural dilemmas of our time. The position has been described with characteristic vigour by Alasdair MacIntyre:[8]

> I do not doubt that in this country there is widespread agreement in condemning murder and theft, just as there is widespread disagreement on capital punishment, divorce and nuclear weapons. What I am equally certain about is that these clear agreements take place against a back-

[8] *Listener*, 26 June 1958.

ground of a larger confusion in our moral thinking. Few of us are able to say to what criteria we ought to appeal in making up our minds; the commonest moral sentiment in public houses and Senior Common Rooms alike is a vague goodwill. Where classical nonconformity found clearly formulated principles in its Bible, where Bentham and James Mill had the test of Utility, we have a miasma of inherited muddle.

In calling it a 'miasma of *inherited* muddle' MacIntyre implies that in order to understand our situation we need to appreciate its history. If Potter cannot now use the word 'duty', it must be because of the word's past associations, and the same is true of Aldington's reaction against 'courage', 'honour', and the rest. The new educational vocabulary has supplanted the old through a process of development which we should be able to trace, and Rees's highly self-conscious manoeuvres with language depend upon his knowledge of an older vocabulary of which he is severely critical but which he is unwilling wholly to repudiate.

Our examples suggest that the muddle arises out of a largely unacknowledged conflict between rival moral theories. If so, it should be possible to identify these and compare them. We should then have a set of ideal types which we could endeavour to express, each in its most defensible form. We should expect to find that each of them tried to swallow the rest, i.e. to explain how the others come to seem plausible and why they must fail nevertheless. It is obvious that the process of comparing these moral theories and, even more, of adjudicating between them will generate its own problems, because it is not clear how one could attain a neutral standpoint, or how, otherwise, one could make a rational choice between them. But let those problems wait their turn.

In the first instance I intend to restrict myself to non-religious theories of morality. I proceed in this way for three main reasons. The first is that, if religious belief does make a difference to ethics, we can discover what this difference is only by looking first at moral conceptions and theories that are not explicitly religious. Whether all of these are as independent of religious beliefs as they are supposed to be is to some extent a matter of controversy, but if any of them require theistic or Christian backing, this is something that needs to be shown. The presumption must be that, where no explicit appeal is made to religion, none is needed.

The second is that a non-religious view of the world is, at least *prima facie,* simpler and more economical than a religous one. Even if a religious explanation turns out in the end to be more satisfying, it must initially appear as a complication. So it is reasonable to approach the phenomenon of morality without preconceptions of a religious kind, and, when we do so, we may find that secular morality is entirely consistent and coherent and so much a matter of general agreement that there is no need to 'bring religion into it'.

Thirdly, in any case most of our contemporaries do in fact approach the subject in this way. This remark is strictly true, of course, only if it is heavily qualified, but it is significant that many would see no need of qualifying it. The 'contemporaries' we have in mind are a restricted selection of those who are living at this time, or even in this country at this time. There are very many people, among them many intelligent and cultivated people, for whom religious belief is at the centre of the moral life; but, on the whole, they do not contribute much to the characteristic intellectual climate of the day. The 'we' of the columnist does not generally include them.

My selection of ideal types is bound to be incomplete, but not, I hope, entirely arbitrary. I shall suggest that contemporary secular humanism has three dominant modes, which I shall call rational humanism, romantic humanism, and liberal humanism. All three are, I believe, extremely potent in the modern imagination. Liberal humanism is, in the Anglo-Saxon world at least, predominant; indeed it can be regarded as the characteristic philosophy of the contemporary British or American intellectual, a status which it owes to its apparent ability to reconcile the other two. I use the word 'philosophy' here in its extended popular sense, but all three types, not surprisingly, have their counterparts in specialist moral philosophy.

Rational humanism maintains 'the possibility of an objective basis for moral theory in terms of an ideal of rational human development'. I take this formulation from the dust-cover of R. Osborn's *Humanism and Moral Theory.*[9] The form and content of rational humanism have varied systematically with changing conceptions of reason, but common to these

[9] George Allen & Unwin (1950).

variations is the insistence that the individual should, at least minimally, discipline his desires in the interest of his own and other people's fulfilment, and that what constitutes man's fulfilment and what conduces to it can be discerned and defended by comparatively straightforward rational procedures in principle available to all and, therefore, binding upon all. Romantic humanism can be seen as a revolt against this entire conception of morality as a rational system claiming authority over the individual and, within the individual, subordinating the will and the emotions to rational control. The character of this revolt in turn has varied in relation to the prevailing type of rational humanism, to which it has been opposed. The relation could, therefore, be described as dialectical; romantics and rationalists have often shared common assumptions (particularly as to the character of 'reason') and differed only as to their proper implications. The romantic typically rejects the claims of reason both in its pretensions to define the ends of life and in its careful control of means; both as regulating the relations between persons and in ordering the individual's inner life; and the reason he rejects is reason as the rationalist currently conceives it.

The history of this dialectical relationship is a great part of the history of modern culture, and to do justice to it would require a full-scale history of ideas. I can only offer a sketch which, though inadequate, will not, I hope, be too misleading.

It was simply a coincidence that I happened to be reading *The Age of Reason* by Jean-Paul Sartre, the first volume of his novel trilogy *The Roads to Freedom,* when I came across in the bookshelf of a cottage in the country a battered copy of *The Age of Reason, being an Investigation of True and Fabulous Theology* by Tom Paine. I was intrigued by the circumstance that two books so strikingly different should share the same title. Was this also a coincidence or could there be some connection between them? I believe I found one: Paine was already contributing to a process of disintegration, which reaches its term in Sartre. Paine's is a naïvely confident rationalism; Sartre's existentialism, despite its Cartesian clarity, is an extreme romantic reaction against the claims of reason.

In Sartre's novel[10] Mathieu is a professor of philosophy in

[10] *The Age of Reason,* translated by Eric Sutton, Penguin (1961).

early middle age. He has been living with a mistress, Marcelle, who now in the seventh year of their association has become pregnant. The plot turns on Mathieu's attempts to raise the money to procure her an abortion, which he is at last reduced to stealing. But before the book ends Marcelle has consented to marry the homosexual Daniel, who sees, as Mathieu does not, that she wants the child. He takes her not out of pity, still less from desire, nor even to embarrass Mathieu, but because 'to do the opposite of what one wants—that is freedom!'

The romantic ambience of the story is evident enough; the characters inhabit a bohemian world in which conventional morality has no place and marriage is contemplated only by the one character who cannot, even if he wished to, give it its traditional significance. Marcelle's abortion and Mathieu's theft are taken for granted as available solutions to their personal predicaments. The power of the book lies not in the story but in Sartre's quite extraordinary psychological insight and devastating accuracy of observation, and in the perverse use he makes of them. He has the art to construct characters who are genuinely and recognizably human and then, having imagined them complete, deprives them by a deliberate act of all that might engage our sympathy.

It is some time before the reader notices what is wrong with these people of Sartre's. They never do anything because they feel they ought to, indeed they never so much as raise the question what they ought to do; they never act out of simple affection. The novel is essentially a philosophical novel and what gives it its peculiar quality is the combination in Sartre of intuitive human sympathy—or empathy—with a theoretical analysis of the nature and necessity of freedom, which, when given expression in his characters, leaves them entirely heartless.

Consider, for example, the passage in which Sartre describes the onset of Mathieu's love for the Russian girl, Ivich. He has just kissed her in a taxi:

> It was love. This time it was love. And Mathieu thought: 'What have I done?' Five minutes ago this love didn't exist; there was between them a rare and precious feeling, without a name and not expressible in gestures. And he had, in fact, made a gesture, the only one that ought not to have been made, it had come spontaneously. A gesture, and this love had appeared before Mathieu, like some insistent and already commonplace entity. Ivich would from now on think that he loved her, she

would think him like the rest: from now on Mathieu would love Ivich, like the other women he had loved—'That wasn't what I wanted of her' he thought with despair. But even by this time he could no longer recall what he had wanted before. Love was there, compact and comfortable, with all its commonplace contrivings, and it was Mathieu who had brought it into being, in absolute freedom. 'It isn't true', he reflected vehemently: 'I don't desire her, I never have desired her'. But he already knew that he was going to desire her. It always finishes like that, he would look at her legs and her breasts, and then, one fine day . . . In a flash he saw Marcelle outstretched on the bed, naked, with her eyes closed: he hated Marcelle'.[11]

Mathieu has by his spontaneous gesture brought 'love' into being, a 'love' which he did not desire, but to which he is now committed. Sartre is obsessively aware of the fact that the individual's thoughts or feelings, once expressed, as they must be if they are to be expressed at all, in public language or overt gesture, are no longer entirely his own. 'Love', once expressed, commits him to a public role and diminishes his freedom. Mathieu aspires after a pure freedom, in which he acts for no reason and from no desire; but paradoxically, just when he thinks he has achieved it, the act frustrates itself by engendering the very commitment he is anxious to avoid.

Since freedom of the Sartrean kind can be won only by disengagement from the claims and demands of others, Sartre's characters do not and cannot enter into personal relationships. As Iris Murdoch puts it in her perceptive essay on Sartre: 'they bump into each other in an external fashion: they are never deeply involved with each other.'[12] 'The individual seen from without is a menace and seen from within is a void.'[13] There is evident, in consequence, an almost complete dissociation of reason, desire and will. Thus:

On the one hand lies the empty reflexion of a reason that has lost faith in its own power to find objective truth, which knows its idea of an unprecarious liberty to be contradictory, and which finds human suffering a scandal and a mystery. On the other lies the dead world of things and conventions, covering up the mute senselessness of the irrational.[14]

The title of Sartre's novel, *The Age of Reason*, may not be entirely ironical. Reason, it suggests, come of age brings us irrevocably to the point at which we can see that life has no

[11] Op. cit., pp. 65–6.
[12] *Sartre, Romantic Rationalist*, Cambridge University Press (1953) p. 33.
[13] p. 80.
[14] p. 82.

meaning beyond what can be given it in the momentary *acte gratuit.* If Sartre still acknowledges reason, it is a reason that has become vacuous and self-destructive. Thus Iris Murdoch sees Sartre as a philosopher 'without the materials to construct a system which will hold and justify [his] values; Sartre believes neither in God nor in Nature nor in History. What he *does* believe in is Reason,'[15] but, in the absence of any coherent metaphysic 'there is no reason why the personage portrayed in *L'Etre et le Néant* should prefer one thing to another or do this rather than that.'[16]

In this, she believes, Sartre exemplifies a characteristically modern predicament:

> When purposes and values are knit comfortably into the neat and small practical activities of life, thought and emotion move together. When this is no longer so, when action involves choosing between worlds, not moving in a world, loving and valuing which were once the rhythm of our lives, become problems.[17]

No doubt a sociological explanation of this state of affairs is, at least up to a point, indicated. The dissociation that Sartre portrays is not a product merely of philosophical speculation, but reflects the pluralism and atomism of an industrial society, in which traditional family and other institutional patterns of the sort that formed and defined the individual's character are steadily eroded, and people become increasingly alienated from the purely contractual systems which have largely supplanted them.[18] But this cannot be the whole story, if only because the cultural trends become apparent earlier than the economic ones. Thought and emotion, Iris Murdoch says, no longer move together. Her language is reminiscent of T. S. Eliot's celebrated essay on the Metaphysical Poets, in which he claimed to discern in the seventeenth century a 'dissociation of sensibility': 'Tennyson and Browing are poets, and they think; but they do not feel their thought as immediately

[15] p. 77. [16] p. 79. [17] p. 33.

[18] Alasdair MacIntyre writes: 'The religion of English society prior to the Industrial Revolution provided a framework within which the metaphysical questions could be asked and answered, even if different and rival answers were given. Who am I? Whence did I come? Whither shall I go? Is there a meaning to my life other than any meaning I choose to give it? What powers govern my fate?' (*Secularization and Moral Change,* Oxford University Press (1967), pp. 29–30.) The Industrial Revolution, he argues, brought with it new class moralities, so that 'there remains no framework within which the metaphysical questions can be systematically asked'.

as the odour of a rose. A thought to Donne was an experience; it modified his sensibility'. And then he generalizes: 'The poets of the seventeenth century, the successors of the dramatists of the sixteenth, possessed a mechanism of sensibility which could devour any kind of experience . . . In the seventeenth century a dissociation of sensibility set in, from which we have never recovered.'[19]

If Eliot was right about this—and his claim has remained controversial—part, at least, of the explanation must lie in the growth of a philosophy which divorced the cognitive powers of men from the rest of the personality and came to define these powers with increasing narrowness. The widest possible claims were made for reason thus narrowly defined and much of what had previously been accepted on the authority of the church or on the strength of revelation was held to be luminously apparent to reason. Less and less remained of a system which could, in Iris Murdoch's phrase 'hold and justify the values' which were nevertheless still to a large extent maintained. An ethic which had developed under the influence of a subtle and complex vision of a natural order subject to and permeated by the supernatural was effectively deprived of its transcendent reference. Where there was still an appeal to nature, it was to a nature whose significance was believed to be written on its face. Often even this appeal was eventually discarded and moral principles were held to be self-evident. For Locke the existence and character of God, the principles of morality and natural rights could all be demonstrated or intuitively apprehended and, although 'truths above reason' were grudgingly admitted, the reasonableness of Christianity left no room for 'enthusiasm'. The development of physical science accelerated this process by encouraging a dualism of mind and body, in which mind was conceived of as active only in speculative inquiry and the emotions and the will were part of man's physical endowment, which he shared with the animals.

Hence Basil Willey takes up and amplifies Eliot's critical theme:

What the cold philosophy did destroy was the union of heart and head,

[19] T. S. Eliot, *Selected Essays,* Faber & Faber (1932), pp. 287–8.

the synthesis of thought and feeling, out of which major poetry seem to be born.[20]

The cleavage began to appear, which has become so troublesomely familiar to us since, between 'values' and 'facts'; between what you *felt* as a human being or as a poet, and what you *thought* as a man of sense, judgement and enlightenment.[21]

And so [Willey notes] by the beginning of the 18th century religion had sunk to deism, while poetry had been reduced to catering for delights—to providing embellishments which might be agreeable to the fancy, but which were recognized by the judgement as having no relation to reality.[22]

Of that 'religion which had sunk to deism' Tom Paine provides a magnificently rumbustious example in the work I mentioned earlier, *The Age of Reason, being an investigation of True and Fabulous Theology.*[23] It was published for the first time in France (and in French) in 1793, 150 years before Sartre's novel of the same title: 'I do not believe', writes Paine, 'in the creed professed by the Jewish Church, by the Roman Church, by the Greek Church, by the Turkish Church, by the Protestant Church, nor by any Church.'[24] And he proceeds to formulate a religion divested of mystery, and based on reason and the moral law:

The Christian mythology has five deities: there is God the Father, God the Son, God the Holy Ghost, the God Providence and the Goddess Nature. But the Christian story of God the Father putting his son to death, or employing people to do it, cannot be told by a parent to a child; and to tell him it was done to make mankind happier and better is making the story still worse as if mankind could be improved by the example of a murder; and to tell him that all this is a mystery is only making an excuse for the incredibility of it. How different is this from the pure and simple profession of deism! The true deist has but one deity; and his religion consists in contemplating the power, wisdom and benignity of the Deity in his works, and in endeavouring to imitate him in everything moral, scientifical and mechanical.[25]

Paine presents us, in effect, with a crude and simplified version of Locke:

Religion, therefore, being the belief of a God and the practice of moral truth, cannot have any connection with mystery. The belief of God, so

[20] Basil Willey, *The Seventeenth Century Background,* Chatto & Windus (1934), p.294.

[21] Op. cit., p. 87.

[22] Ibid.

[23] Thinker's Library, Watts & Co. (1938).

[24] Op. cit., p. 2.

[25] Op. cit., pp. 41f.

far from having anything of mystery in it, is of all beliefs the most easy, because it arises to us, as it is observed, out of necessity.[26]

Man has only to follow carefully the instructions of 'the Almighty Lecturer': 'The Almighty Lecturer, by displaying the principles of science in the structure of the universe, has invited man to study and to imitation.'[27] Reason for Paine, and in this he is characteristic of the Enlightenment, was the faculty by which men learned the principles of science and of morals. The principle of the uniformity of nature was intuitively evident as were the precepts of the moral law. The existence of God was demonstrable. Here was a religion within the bounds of reason which justified the laws of nature and the Rights of Man, and made no concessions to mystery or enthusiasm.

Paine was a brilliant pamphleteer and propagandist, but he was not an original thinker. For this very reason he provides a lively and not altogether unjust caricature of the tenor of philosophy from Descartes by way of Locke to the French Enlightenment. What all these had done was to narrow the connotation of 'reason' while making the widest possible claims for its competence. Everything that mattered for human life could be comprehended by thinking and by thinking of a special kind, the kind that is done by mathematicians (or by natural scientists, thought of as applied mathematicians). The hosts of Reason had thus become a thin line stretched out to defend a vast territory over a wide front and eminently vulnerable to attack.

The attack came from David Hume, who at the time Paine wrote had already defined the limits of the sort of mathematical thinking, for which, under the name of reason, Paine had claimed so much. Matters of fact could not be demonstrated; the uniformity of nature could not be proved; that God exists can only be an article of faith; and, in matters of conduct 'reason is and ought to be the slave of the passions'.

In his writings Hume disposed of both the forms of rational humanism that had dominated the eighteenth century, that which based morality on a rational pattern immanent in and discernible in the world of nature; and that which based it on principles intuitively evident to reason. The first task was

[26] Op. cit., p. 51.

[27] Op. cit., p. 32.

discharged in the *Dialogues of Natural Religion,* the second in *The Treatise of Human Nature.*

Henceforward, anyone who wanted to 'argue for the possibility of an objective basis for moral theory in terms of an ideal of rational human development' (to use Osborn's phraseology again) would have to be thoroughly empirical and base it on science or common sense. Hence the characteristically modern type of rational humanism is the scientific humanism which has as its philosophical counterpart some kind of utilitarianism.

2

Rational Humanism

It is difficult to give an account of scientific humanism which is not open to the objection that one is setting up a man of straw. And perhaps there is no thinker, at any rate no professional philosopher, of distinction who would accept this title. Yet, as a tendency, it has been and still is enormously influential. Its general tone emerges from Dr Alec Comfort's explanation of his aims in his book *Sex and Society*:

> The view put forward here is based on the form of rationalism and humanism which seems to the author closest to the general spirit of experimental science: that no form of sexual behaviour can be regarded as unacceptable, sinful, or deserving of censure unless it has demonstrable ill effects on the individual who practises it or on others.[1]

Formally speaking this is a variety of utilitarianism: what is right or wrong is to be determined by consequences. As J. J. C. Smart remarks of utilitarianism: 'With its empirical attitude to questions of means and ends it is congenial to the scientific temper and it has flexibility to deal with a changing world.'[2] It is open to a utilitarian, while regarding the nature of the consequences as the sole criterion of right action, to insist that he adopts this criterion simply from personal choice and to reserve to himself the decision as to how it shall be interpreted. But this is an uncharacteristic posture for the scientific humanist, for the whole tendency of his position is towards the substitution of scientific authority for private judgement. Comfort himself is, as it happens, an individualist who insists upon the authority of personal decision, but it is apparent from his discussion how difficult it is in practice to prevent its being continuously eroded by the claims of science. In order to fulfil the task allotted to it by the scientific humanist, research in the social sciences must concern itself with

[1] *Sex and Society,* Penguin (1964), p. 15.

[2] *Utilitarianism For and Against,* by J. J. C. Smart and Bernard Williams, Cambridge University Press (1973), p. 73.

discovering the most reliable means to the achievement of certain desirable ends or the avoidance of certain undesirable ones. Who is to decide which goals are desirable and which undesirable? No doubt the layman could in principle decide what are desirable goals, but it is not he who designs and carries out experiments or other empirical investigations, but the scientists themselves. It is they who have to determine what they shall measure and what the scale of measurement shall be, and, since science can deal best with what is measurable, any desirable goal tends so far as practicable to be quantified, and initial caution against identifying the originally selected goal with what is thus quantified is almost inevitably disregarded. Thus one index of a satisfactory sexual relationship is, no doubt, the attainment of simultaneous orgasm. This, being susceptible of measurement, is intensively studied by e.g. Masters and Johnson, and the results are offered as scientifically validated studies of sexual compatibility. But when the layman wants a harmonious sexual relationship, he wants a good deal more than this.

An even more familiar example is the use of intelligence tests. The purpose of such tests is usually to help determine whether people are suitable for academic work: that is to say whether they are intelligent in the sense of being good reasoners. But to measure (as distinct from to judge or assess) good reasoning is extremely difficult. You can measure how often someone has got the right answer, but not, outside of formal logic and pure mathematics, whether he got it for the right reason. And if the candidate is intelligent enough to see that the question is ambiguous or admits of more than one right answer, he suffers a distinct handicap in this type of test. If the aim is, so far as possible, to *develop* intelligence, and you measure intelligence so as to discover how far you are successful, it will make a decisive difference whether what you are in fact measuring is what you really want to develop. Hence the tough-minded proposal to define intelligence as the 'sum of what intelligent tests measure' does not meet the case.[3] Teachers in schools and universities will be familiar with examples of research into the effectiveness of teaching

[3] Cf. John Wilson, *Philosophy and Educational Research,* NFER (1972), pp. 31–2 and chapter 6.

methods, which are subject to similar displacement.

It should, one might think, be easy to guard against these distortions but even in theory there are difficulties in doing so. Once the primacy of the scientific approach is accepted, almost every activity of any significance, however personal, falls within the domain of the appropriate expert: child-rearing, education, sex and marriage, punishment. The layman is confident indeed who feels he can afford to dispense with expert help; but when help is offered it is, naturally, what the expert regards as help in relation to what the expert sees as the problem. The layman who insists that it is for him to judge whether what the scientist conceives of as desirable *is* desirable has to face the charge that he is relying upon nothing more dependable than pre-scientific common sense. And it is the admitted inadequacies of such a guide that prompted the recourse to science in the first place. The layman is liable to be told that what he takes to be knowledge is not knowledge at all but mere subjective opinion.

It is, as it happens, not difficult to distinguish between what the sexologist studies, viz. such things as the attainment of simultaneous orgasm and what the layman is interested in, viz. a harmonious sexual relationship, and one is normally a component of the other; but as a branch of science becomes more developed such discriminations become harder to make. It is, for instance, far from easy to say what *is* the relationship between our ordinary concept of intelligence and whatever it is that intelligence tests measure. Bearing these problems in mind, let us consider Comfort's statement of the aims of the sexual sociologist:

> At the present time the public turns increasingly to science for the solution of its problems, because it rightly expects that the difficulties individuals and societies encounter in ordering their relationships will prove capable of being tackled by modifications of the method that has brought such eminently successful results in practical issues, such as disease control, and in theoretical problems of ultimate practical interest, such as solar physics. Having the opportunity and the responsibility to remove the whole question of sexual behaviour, which has always proved troublesome to human societies to a greater or lesser degree, from the field of conjecture and myth into the field of observational research, we should be wrong to refuse to intervene in matters of social ethics.[4]

To intervene effectually, however, Comfort argues, we need

[4] Op. cit., pp. 18–19.

to know four things: how human beings behave sexually in our own and other cultures; which patterns of behaviour are associated with abnormality or maladjustment, or have undesirable effects on the participants or on others; what patterns of conduct can be upheld with confidence as a general aim—the analogue of a balanced diet in the study of nutrition; what types of education and social facilities will make the realization of such an optimum pattern possible. Comfort does not discuss at any length the question which is of central importance for utilitarianism, viz. *what* effects one should be seeking to produce. Traditional answers have been pleasure, satisfaction, happiness. In this particular passage he seems to regard the avoidance of 'abnormality' or 'maladjustment' as being bad in themselves, to be distinguished from 'undesirable effects'. Perhaps, however he would wish to avoid them only because of their tendency to produce unhappiness in those affected. Yet the analogy with a balanced diet seems to imply some criterion of what the organism needs which is not to be identified simply with what the individual happens to want or what he believes would give him pleasure or make him happy. If he presupposes such a criterion, he is in line with other humanists who tend to assimilate morality to what produces physical and mental health. It is easy to see how this view favours expert opinion.[5]

Generally speaking Comfort assumes that conflict of any kind is among the undesirable consequences that the sociologist will seek to remove, whether it is conflict within the individual or between the individual and society. There are problems here (which Comfort recognizes) about the best way to resolve such conflicts—especially those between the individual and society—but, quite apart from these, the layman may not agree in any particular case that absence of conflict is desirable or that it is an overriding aim; and he may not agree with the expert as to what constitutes absence of conflict. Moreover what counts as conflict is often to some extent a matter of convention, as anyone will know who has listened to a group of Greeks in a *taverna* amicably engaged in settling the time and place for their next meeting.

[5] Cf. Hector Hawton, *The Humanist Revolution,* Barrie & Rockliff (1963), p. 140; Walter Lippman, *Preface to Morals,* George Allen & Unwin (1929), p. 175.

There are, then even in theory, strong tendencies in scientific humanism which inhibit the exercise of personal judgement on moral questions, and they manifest themselves even in a confessed individualist like Comfort. But there are reasons why, however strongly it is maintained that the final decision in matters of value rests with the individual, it is difficult or impossible to make that decision effective in practice. For, as a matter of fact, research in the social sciences at any given time is carried on within a particular set of assumptions about value. Hence its results are largely unavailable to anyone who does not share those values or does not wholly share them. He could, of course, in principle, unpick, so to speak, the skein of research and realign the threads in the direction of the goals he himself regards as important, but he often cannot do so in practice and he might well find, if he tried it, that research designed to answer one set of questions would give little or no help in answering others. So that unless and until he is able to undertake the massive task of shifting the entire emphasis of current research he is virtually unable to gain scientific backing for his intuitive judgements. Meanwhile these judgements, *because* they lack scientific backing, are liable to be dismissed as 'subjective'. His position is not unlike that of the private objector at a planning tribunal who faces an official proposal backed by an enormous wealth of detailed investigation. He may, if lucky, be able to use some of the official figures to support his own case, but to the extent that they do so, it will be accidentally, since it was not for that purpose that they were compiled.

Although it is not, perhaps, inevitable that the social sciences should accept the value judgements which in fact do guide their operation at any particular time, nevertheless once entrenched it is difficult to dislodge them, since they are almost inextricably built into the foundations of the discipline in its existing form and share its prestige. There is, in particular, one feature which belongs to the utilitarian structure of scientific humanism and determines the questions to which research is addressed and thus the answers it is possible to give: the concentration upon desirable or undesirable consequences. This of itself tends to divert attention from considerations which the layman may well judge important, but which do not readily fit into the means-end pattern. Thus Comfort remarks in relation to monogamy:

The prevalent conception of marriage, both in the law and in the religious code, insists that any act of sexual intercourse by either party with a third is ground for censure . . . Without overrating the human desire for variety, which is at least partially counter-poised by a desire for stability, it seems clear that this view is not essentially a part of monogamy, and if we accept reproductive monogamy as a standard, we must base our judgements on the significance of fidelity on its effects on the stability of the home.[6]

As Comfort recognizes, fidelity is essential to the prevalent conception of marriage or, at least, the traditional conception. When he says that 'it is not essentially a part of monogamy' he means, I think, two things. First, that one could and does find monogamy without this insistence—where it is understood, for example, that either party may take a lover without disturbing the marriage. Second, that the presence or absence of this feature does not significantly affect its character as a monogamous marriage; and whether the institution of monogamous marriage is better or worse for its presence is to be decided entirely by its effects on the stability of the home. Research can, in principle, determine this question. It is possible that problems would arise at this stage, of the sort we have already noted, in deciding what is to count as stability, but, given agreement on this, there is the more fundamental difficulty that many are not content to grant fidelity a merely instrumental value in the way Comfort proposes. They have an ideal of marriage as a sacramental union in which mutual fidelity is of the essence and, for them, to fail of fidelity would be properly a ground of censure calling for forgiveness, even if the stability of the marriage was unaffected.

Faced by such an attitude, and remembering his commitment to 'remove the whole question of sexual behaviour . . . from the field of conjecture and myth into the field of observational research' and thus to 'intervene in social ethics', Comfort's sexual sociologist is bound to stigmatize this ideal of fidelity as irrational and to seek by education and other means to eliminate it.

At this point a further feature of this whole approach

[6] *Sex and Society*, p. 116.

becomes apparent. Comfort's programme necessarily has to be a radical one, insasmuch as the benefits of scientific social research can often not be made available to people as they are, but only to people as they might be, if their attitudes were appropriately redirected by education. Two tendencies in scientific humanism here coalesce, the reliance on experts and the commitment to what Karl Popper has called 'utopian social engineering'. That these tendencies are apparent in the field of education today cannot be denied. The expert educationalist knows better than the parent what is good for the child and what the child should become if he is to benefit from all that he is offered. Similarly he knows better than the teacher how to teach and how to maintain discipline, indeed how much discipline ought to be maintained. And the credentials of the expert are provided by scientific research. Professor R. S. Peters recognizes and goes some way towards explaining this state of affairs:

In England we are developing a highly differentiated society . . . without a common culture and shared ideals. This should not surprise us; for where are such unifying ideals to be fostered? The study of literature, history and the classics has had to be cut down to make room for the vast expansion in scientific education, and the Church is rapidly losing the authority it once had as the source of unifying ideals. We tend to treat the doctor who looks after our bodies and the psychiatrist who looks after our minds with more respect than we treat the priest who advises us about our souls – if we still think we have one. For they are scientists; and it is scientists who are now coming to be thought of as repositories of wisdom about the mysteries of life. . . . This general trend explains why the educationalist sometimes inclines his ear towards a new expert, the psychologist, when he is at a loss to find new unifying educational ideals to replace the old religious ones. There is thus much talk in educational circles of 'the mental health of the child', 'wholeness', 'integration', 'adjustment' and all that sort of thing.[7]

A manifestation of this process is the massive change in educational language which is illustrated in the Educational Bulletin quoted earlier.[8] The words in the second list express a radically different conception of the aims of education from those in the first and for this reason no direct translation from one to the other is possible. It would, in principle, be possible

[7] *Aims in Education*, ed. T. H. B. Hollins, Manchester University Press (1964), p. 71.

[8] p. 5 above.

(though in practice rather difficult) to make explicit the psychological and sociological theories underlying the new language. This language is likely to change still further for two reasons.

One is that science develops, so that what is regarded as scientific knowledge at one period is subject to more or less considerable revision later. The other is that, as we have seen, the value judgements implicit in the social sciences of a particular period may themselves subsequently alter. These reasons help to explain the striking role of fashion in the social sciences. Whatever the experts said yesterday they are emphatically repudiating today and what they will say tomorrow heaven alone knows.[9] Peters made his comment in 1964 and it may well be that different language is now in vogue from that of wholeness, integration, and adjustment. The phenomenon is not confined to the social sciences, but is endemic in all academic pursuits. It is, perhaps, best (and most charitably) understood as a necessary part of the process by which alternative possibilities of development are worked out and tested. And, in a curious zig-zag pattern, genuine progress is made. But it justifies a certain reserve on the part of the layman in allowing his more important decisions to be too much influenced by expert opinion. In child-rearing, for example, consistency is to be sought above all else; hence the mother who brings up her child by the light of common sense is more likely to be successful than the one who follows the latest theory, for this will change more than once before the child reaches maturity. Dr Spock's 'recantation' is remarkable only in its honesty and in the public attention it received.

If the scientific humanist's programme necessarily has to be radical in this way, it is exposed to the criticism most effectively expressed by Popper, that we simply do not have, and are unlikely ever to have, the sort and degree of knowledge about the effects of our actions that would justify the radical policies proposed. We are in fact much more likely to

[9] Until very recently it was commonly assumed among criminologists that the chief aim of punishment was the reformation or rehabilitation of the offender, and research was largely directed to discovering the most effective means of integrating him into society. This assumption is now being challenged under the influence of radical politics. Society, it is now being claimed, has no right to alter the offender's attitudes, even by persuasion, but only to require him to submit to penalties.

do harm than good if we try to introduce large-scale changes based, as they would have to be, upon our very limited understanding. It is not hard to document Popper's objection. There seemed to be, at the time, sound theoretical reasons of a sociological kind for assuming that housing estates in the form of high-rise buildings would provide a healthy and attractive environment for the families of slum-dwellers. High density of occupation could be achieved while at the same time large expanses of uncluttered open space could be provided. It has taken less than a generation to discover that the experts were tragically mistaken. Similarly the construction of urban motorways on the basis of a scientific assessment of traffic needs has had unforeseen consequences for the quality of life in the adjacent areas.

Popper himself favours 'piece-meal social engineering', which concentrates on identifying and removing palpable evils rather than promoting large scale goods, and in this he is wise. But this concession to good sense severely limits the scope of scientific humanism by favouring short-term decisions which must largely accept men as they are with their generally unenlightened preferences and prejudices. And it is hard to see how it can be a matter for scientific judgement to determine whether and to what extent people's unreasoned preferences and prejudices should be respected.

It is only, I suggest, by reflection upon these tendencies in scientific humanism that one can appreciate the enormous and entirely unpredicted reaction that has occurred among sections of the young against the scientific elements in our culture (itself a striking example of the inability of sociologists to detect even short-term social trends). Otherwise it is hard to credit that the serious and high-minded advocates of scientific humanism could attract such apparently ill-merited abuse. This reaction is a further phase of the dialectic between romantic and rational humanism, and draws much of its strength from the earlier romantic tradition. Seen from this romantic standpoint the ideal society of scientific humanism is the 'technocracy' which Theodore Roszak defines as follows: '. . . that society in which those who govern justify themselves by appeal to technical experts who, in turn, justify themselves by appeal to scientific forms of knowledge. And beyond the authority of science there is no appeal.'[10] What Roszak calls 'this grand cultural imperative' has three premisses:

1. That the vital needs of man are purely technical in character. If a problem does not have a technical solution, it is not a real problem.
2. That, in the technocracy, where the authorities are so well intentioned and well informed, any remaining friction must be due to a 'breakdown in communication'. Hence 'in all walks of life, image makers and public relations specialists assume greater and greater prominence. The regime of experts relies on a lieutenancy of counterfeiters who seek to integrate the discontent born of thwarted aspiration by way of clever falsification.'[11]
3. The experts 'who have fathomed our heart's desire and who alone can continue providing for our needs are the *certified* experts financed by the state or corporate structure'.

As an account of the way modern society is actually organized there is some exaggeration here, but it is scarcely a parody of the stated ideals of scientific humanism. Indeed, we have become so familiar with the warnings of *Brave New World* and *1984* that it is hard for us now to recapture the enthusiasm with which the prospect of a scientifically oriented society was greeted little more than a generation ago by Walter Lippman (writing in 1929):

> The full realization of the place of science in modern life came slowly, and only in our generation can it be said that political rulers, captains of industry and leaders of thought have actually begun to appreciate how central is science in our civilization, and to act upon that realization. In our time governments have begun to take science seriously . . . Great corporations have established laboratories of their own . . . Money has become available in great quantities for scientific work in the universities...
>
> The motives and habits of mind which are thus brought into play at the very heart of modern civilization are mature and disinterested. That may not be the primary intention, but it is the inevitable result . . . This is an original and tremendous fact in human experience: that a whole civilization should be dependent upon technology, that this technology should be dependent upon pure science, and that this pure science should be dependent upon a race of men who consciously refuse, as Mr. Bertrand Russell has said, to regard their 'own desires, tastes and

[10] *The Making of a Counter Culture,* Faber & Faber (1970), p. 8.
[11] Op. cit., p. 15.

interests as affording a key to the understanding of the world.[12]

This latest version of rational humanism shares with its predecessors (which, of course, continue to influence some minds, so that the varieties continue to coexist) the tendency to narrow the scope of reason while making ambitious claims for its competence. Reason for the scientific humanist is to be identified with scientific method and with the process by which effective means are selected for the achievement of given ends. Revolt against such conceptions could take one of two forms: refusal to limit the scope of reason in the ways proposed; or rejection of the claims of reason altogether—it being assumed that reason was being correctly defined. The romantic movement has exemplified both forms, but it is the latter which has predominated and which I propose to characterize as romantic humanism.

In this development Kant was a turning-point. He recognized and accepted the Humean critique of the metaphysical reasoning by which men had sought to prove the existence of God, freedom, and immortality and claimed this as a liberation of morality:

> So far as morality is based upon the conception of man as a free agent who, just because he is free, binds himself through his reason to unconditional laws, it stands in need neither of the idea of another Being over him, for him to apprehend his duty, nor of an incentive other than the law itself, for him to do his duty. At least it is man's own fault if he is subject to such a need; and, if he is, this need can be relieved through nothing outside himself: for whatever does not originate in himself and in his own freedom in no way compensates for the deficiency of his morality. Hence for its own sake morality does not need religion at all (whether objectively, as regards willing, or subjectively, as regards ability [to act]); by virtue of pure practical reason it is self-sufficient.[13]

So far as religion was concerned, his policy was 'to deny knowledge to make room for faith'. But he sought to provide a rational foundation for morality, which he himself regarded as so secure that he reintroduced God, freedom, and immortality as presuppositions of morality. It is evidence of the remarkable persistence of the teleological idea that Kant was not wholly consistent in his rejection of metaphysics and

[12] *Preface to Morals*, pp. 237–8.

[13] *Religion within the Limits of Reason Alone*, translated by T. M. Greene and H. H. Hudson, 2nd edn., Harper (1960), p. 3.

covertly appealed to the concept of nature in his formulation of the categorical imperative. It is only by claiming that *the function* of self-love is to preserve life that he can discern a 'contradiction of the will' in the maxim of the intending suicide: and it is only by maintaining that our talents have been 'given us' for self-improvement that he can stigmatize as immoral the man who proposes to allow his talents to remain undeveloped. For, as he readily concedes, we can easily conceive a situation in which everyone commits suicide or lives like the lotus-eaters. And even the refusal of help to others is, in his terms, a breach of the categorical imperative, only if the individual 'wills' to be helped himself. If he can refuse to be helped himself, he is not inconsistent in refusing help to others. If, however, he cannot refuse to be helped himself, it must be because, in the nature of the case, he needs help. And this involves a moral justification of a basically teleological kind.

Once Kant's system is deprived of these illicit supports it becomes evident that contrary axioms can together satisfy the requirement that the will should not contradict itself, so that reason as Kant understands it no longer suffices to justify the choice of one alternative rather than another. All that it requires is that the agent be prepared to be consistent in his choices and make the same demands upon himself as upon anyone else similarly situated. There is no longer any basis for objectivity in ethics of the kind Kant took for granted. Once this is recognized, however, a man may feel that he can still avoid 'heteronomy'; he can still refuse to yield to 'pathological' desire or to defer to a tradition with which he has not freely identified himself; and, if he succeeds in this, he avoids bad faith and achieves an inner integrity or authenticity, which becomes for him the supreme value. The use of this language shows how easily post-Kantian moral reflection merges into existentialism (and, of course, the influence of Kant upon Sartre is manifest).

Kant is himself a rationalist, indeed the culmination of the Enlightenment deification of reason; for the regulative role of reason is absolute as exemplified in the categorical imperative; but it is purely regulative, since reason is now without content. Every consideration (except the appeal to nature) which might provide us with reasons for preferring one consistent course of action to another has been carefully eliminated. So here reason is at once at its least substantial and most authoritative. Kant believed that he was providing a rational basis for traditional ethics all the more secure for its openly dispensing with insecure metaphysical props. But why should one maintain this abstract framework of rational control? Or, if one maintains it, why not subordinate it to the satisfaction of desire? The Kantian system has made restraint pointless and, by its emphasis upon the freedom and autonomy of the individual, has encouraged him to create his own values. Kantian man is restrained by reason, no doubt, but he is freed from all other restraints, except in so far as he chooses to accept them. The message is plain; a man should be himself as fully and freely as he can. There are no models to imitate save those which are self-chosen and self-imposed. Once men are freed from the authority of God and the constraints of human nature it is not surprising that authenticity, spontaneity and creativity become the dominant values, and these are the values of what I am calling 'romantic humanism'. It can be seen both as a development from and as a protest against the austere rationalism of Kant. A tidy logical coherence is not to be looked for in it, but there is an intelligible, if loose, relationship between its various manifestations.

3

Romantic Humanism

It was characteristic of the varieties of rationalism that prevailed in the eighteenth century that they favoured universality, objectivity, clarity, order, and deliberation. The revolt against them concentrated with varying degrees of emphasis upon what is unique to the individual or to the nation, what is subjective, mysterious, spontaneous, and unrestrained. Its ideal is the free, independent, and creative individual, who is characteristically a rebel against tradition and a subverter of institutions, who spends himself and others in his search for depth of experience and authentic self expression. Not all of these attitudes are opposed to every kind of rationalism. Indeed the newer scientific form of rational humanism has lent support to the demand for creativity—to such an extent that John Weightman is prepared to trace the concept of the avant-garde to the influence of science: '[The avant-garde] . . . is basically connected with science, and with what is sometimes called the scientific revolution, the replacement of the medieval belief in a finished universe by the modern scientific view of a universe evolving in time'.[1] But scientists themselves are in a position to develop a cumulative understanding of the natural world, whereas artists enjoy no such opportunity. The artist may, significantly, engage in constant 'experiment', but there are no accepted means of validating his results. Romantic humanism, therefore, takes over the creative, but not the critical, emphasis of science. Indeed in some recent forms it has tended to repudiate the scientific world-view altogether on the ground that it reduces man and nature to the status of mere objects.

It is characteristic of scientific humanism to maintain that it is in principle possible to solve ethical problems given enough empirical knowledge. It follows *a fortiori* that, for the scientific humanist, if two people disagree about a point of morals

[1] *The Concept of the Avant-Garde,* Alcove Press (1973), p. 20.

at least one of them must be mistaken—even if, in our present state of knowledge, we cannot tell which one that is. That is to say, scientific humanism is objectivist as also were the older forms of rational humanism. None of them is prepared to envisage ultimate and irreconcilable disagreement in matters of right or wrong, although of course, people may in fact continue to differ, since men are both fallible and wilful. Morality is a rational construction which can be given, in principle at least, a scientific basis. Because of this it applies to everyone, even if not everyone is prepared to recognize it.

The romantic humanist, by contrast, rejects the restraints that such an objective morality would impose upon his individual creativity and freedom. Once it is conceded that it is possible, if only in principle, to discern by some rational process what is right or wrong, the individual is, he feels, to that extent in fetters. His will is no longer sovereign and he has no alternative but to 'nurse unacted desires' (to use William Blake's phrase). Sincerity and spontaneity are forfeit, because there is an inevitable hypocrisy in following the demands of objective duty when, as must often happen, one's deepest inclination is to do otherwise. How can a man 'be himself' when required to subscribe to an ethic which does not proceed from his own soul? The romantic's model is the unattached artist who is prepared to subordinate the interests of others, even his own interest, to the development of his genius. As Weightman writes:

> It has long been axiomatic in France that the artist has to be a rebel, an outcast, a demolisher of old forms, a hater of the bourgeoisie, an exceptional individual who lives according to his private anticipation of the laws of the perfect society of the future, not according to the *defective* rules of existing society.[2]

Accordingly the romantic humanist is committed to a subjectivist moral philosophy; either that or the rejection of morality altogether. By 'subjectivism' I mean the contradictory of 'objectivism': the view that it is *not* the case that if two people contradict one another on a point of morals at least one of them must be mistaken.[3] In using the expression 'at least one

[2] Weightman, op. cit., p. 29.

[3] In wishing to make use of this distinction I am reassured by Mr J. L. Mackie's discussion of it in his *Ethics: Inventing Right and Wrong*, Penguin (1977), pp. 22-5.

of them must be mistaken' I intend something stronger than 'one cannot consistently agree with both'. To be an objectivist is to hold that whether something is or is not morally right is independent of the attitudes or inclinations of any particular speaker or set of speakers. It is to deny what Professor R. M. Hare explicitly asserts, that 'all moral arguments are *ad hominem*'.[4] The terms 'subjective' and 'objective' have been used variously in the history of moral philosophy and I would not use them if I could think of better ones to mark the distinction that I have in mind. As I use them, the terms 'objective' and 'subjective' exhaust the field; and they are, of course, mutually exclusive. The term 'objective' has in the past been applied to the doctrine that saying that anything is good or right we are mentioning a property which it has, the property of goodness or rightness. A typical objectivist, according to this usage, is G. E. Moore, who held that the word 'good' stands for a unique, unanalysable, simple property, on the analogy of 'yellow'; though, unlike yellow, it is a 'non-natural' property. The term 'subjective' has often been applied to the doctrine that it is the sole function of moral judgements to describe or express the speaker's feelings. When 'objective' and 'subjective' are understood in these ways they do not, of course, exhaust the field. A theory may be neither objectivist nor subjectivist. Hare's moral philosophy, for example, is not in any sense objectivist; but equally it is not subjectivist in this sense. However, few philosophers would now advocate either objectivism or subjectivism in these narrower senses, which makes it easier to drop them quickly and continue to use the words in a way that does mark an important distinction.

The essential claim of subjectivism, so understood, is that morality is constituted by the principles or the attitudes which an individual adopts, freely and responsibly, as his answer to the question, 'How shall I live?' Its central contention is that moral disagreement can always be analysed into two components: (i) disagreement about the facts; (ii) disagreement in values (sometimes called 'disagreement in attitude'). Disagreement about the facts is, in principle, resolvable. Disagreement in values may be ultimate. It follows that a moral argument may always break down, because even should the disputants

[4] *Freedom and Reason*, Clarendon Press (1963), p. 111.

come to agree about the facts, there is no guarantee of their achieving agreement in attitude or any reason, ultimately, why they should. And once the issue of fact is settled, there is no rational way of settling the moral point. As Sir Alfred Ayer once put it, crudely but concisely, 'I lay down one rule and you lay down another and the issue betwen us is a subject for persuasion and finally a matter for individual choice'.[5] For romantic humanism therefore, to repeat Iris Murdoch's words, it is always the case that 'action involves choosing between worlds, not moving in a world'.

There are, as we shall see later, technical considerations of logic which influenced philosophers of the analytic tradition in arriving at this position. Nevertheless, the correspondence with the diffused romanticism of literature and the arts is striking. In his book, *The Characters of Love,* Professor John Bayley refers to Hume's remark that all men agree to tread on the pavement instead of upon their fellows' toes:

> Does such an agreement still exist? In life obviously it does; for purposes of daily convenience we still agree not to tread on each other's toes, but is there any comparable agreement in the world of the writer? Do we and Proust tacitly agree that toe-treading is wrong? On the contrary, it is an article of faith today that nothing shall be taken for granted between reader and author; we must submit ourselves to the purity of his insight and accept or reject it in the isolation of our own responses.[6]

Both developments betray a cultural situation in which the 'cleavage between fact and values', to which Basil Willey referred is taken for granted. And this is influenced by a pervasive assumption that 'facts' are the preserve of science and common sense. The question for moral philosophy then becomes 'can values be derived from facts so understood?': the 'naturalist' maintains that they can; the 'non-naturalist' that they cannot.

The most rigorously worked out form of what I am calling 'subjectivism' is the 'prescriptivism' of Professor R. M. Hare as it was presented in *The Language of Morals.*[7] In *Freedom and Reason* and his more recent work Hare has modified and developed his doctrine in such a way that it can no longer be

[5] *Polemic,* 1947, p. 30.
[6] Constable (1960), pp. 276–7.
[7] Clarendon Press (1952).

taken as the philosophical equivalent of romantic humanism.[8] But his earlier position is still, I think, that which a romantic humanist would have to adhere to if he wished to defend his position against philosophical criticism.

According to this view, when we call an action, a character or a situation of 'good', it is necessary to distinguish between the meaning of the word 'good' which is given by its use as a term of commendation, i.e. its 'evaluative meaning', and the criteria for the application of the word, which consist in those characteristics in virtue of which the agent resolves to commend the action, character or situation, its 'descriptive meaning'. The criteria specified, the 'descriptive meaning', will vary with the moral code of the agent; the commendatory function of the word, its 'evaluative meaning' remains constant. A request for reasons for calling something 'good' is to be met by indicating the characteristics in virtue which I commend it.

Similarly with decisions. If called upon to justify a decision, I must refer to the principle upon which it was based; and, if called upon to justify that, I must indicate the consequences of the universal application of the principle (for it is these consequences which provide the principle with its content). And so, as Hare points out, we could ultimately be driven back to 'a complete specification of the way of life of which the (original) principle is part'. And he goes on to say: 'This complete specification it is impossible in practice to give; the nearest attempts are those given by the great religions, especially those which can point to historical persons who carried out the way of life in practice.'[9] Moral vocabulary is, of course, very much richer than the discussion so far suggests. It is not restricted to 'good' and 'bad', 'right' and 'wrong'. We have only to turn to some of the examples given earlier.[10] In the two lists of words in educational use there occur, on the one side, 'duty', 'wicked', 'scholar', 'naughty'; on the other side

[8] In chapter 4 I shall suggest that Hare's present position has affinities with 'liberal humanism'. Hare would not, I think, agree that the later book does more than draw out the implications of the earlier one (see *Freedom and Reason,* p. 200); but in *The Language of Morals* the account of moral reasoning developed in Parts II and III of *Freedom and Reason* was left incomplete. Hence it remained unclear by what rational process a choice could be made between principles, each of which was prescriptive and universalizable.

[9] *The Language of Morals,* Clarendon Press (1952), pp. 68f.

[10] In chapter I, pp. 4–6 above.

'anti-social', 'uncooperative', 'creative', 'open-ended'. To the first list one could add all the words for traditional virtues and vices: 'honesty', 'dishonesty', 'courage', 'benevolence', 'malice', etc.

The prescriptivist regards it as a strength in his theory that he can apply it to these words also, in such a way as to explain how the transition can take place from the one list to the other. For a word's evaluative meaning may alter, while its descriptive meaning remains the same, or vice versa; in some words the evaluative meaning is primary, in others the descriptive. Potter, we may remember, was unhappy about the 'weird associations' that the word 'duty' had accumulated—to such an extent, indeed, that he was reluctant to use it.[11] A word may become so polluted that it must be carefully sterilized before it is fit for circulation again. All these cases can be accommodated once it is recognized that every such word has, so to speak, its evaluative and descriptive components. Thus the word 'duty' tends to be associated with the performance of a role. My 'duty' is typically my duty as a soldier, a doctor, a member of Parliament, a father, a husband; and such duties in a stable society are comparatively fixed and unalterable. That is to say the criteria for the application of the word 'duty' are comparatively inflexible. Given this situation someone like Potter who, we may suppose, dislikes the social order in which the concept of duty is, (or was), embedded has two courses open to him. He may try to detach 'duty' from its existing criteria and talk, for example, of the individual's 'duty' to criticize the institutions under which he lives; or, if these criteria are too strong for him—if the 'descriptive meaning' remains obstinately primary—he must give up the use of this word and look for another, when he wants to be prescriptive. He may, of course, still find it convenient to use the word in what Hare calls its 'inverted comma sense': 'Do your "duty" if you must, but you forfeit my respect.' So Gareth Rees in his letter to *The Times* sees more 'old-fashioned good Christianity' in his trendy comprehensive than in 'any religious, excellent, patriotic, single-sex, single-caste establishment'. 'Excellent' is used in the inverted-comma sense; for clearly Rees himself does not commend that kind of school.

[11] Quoted on p. 5 above.

The Underlying process is described by Hare:

> Moral principles or standards are first established; then they get too rigid, and the words used in referring to them becomes too dominantly descriptive; their evaluative force has to be painfully revived before the standards are out of danger. In the course of revival, the standards get adapted to changed circumstances; moral reform takes place, and its instrument is the evaluative use of value-language. The remedy, in fact, for moral stagnation and decay is to learn to use our value-language for the purpose for which it is designed; and this involves not merely a lesson in talking, but a lesson in doing that which we commend; for unless we are prepared to do this we are doing no more than pay lip-service to a conventional standard.[12]

Morality changes, we are given to understand, through individuals or groups coming to commend or condemn different things and modifying language by the various devices we have noticed, and others, so that it is fitted to express these new valuations. And it is a corollary of this process that incompatible moral attitudes compete for our approval and acceptance.

But how is the individual to adjudicate between these rival moralities? So long as each of them is internally consistent there is, apparently, no reason why he should prefer one to another. 'Moralities' (the plural here is natural) are invested with a sort of impermeability. Taking their origin in the individual's resolve to live in a certain way, they can find their ultimate justification only in the resolve which created them and, if other people choose to resolve otherwise, there is no way of settling the dispute. Hare makes this explicit in the passage quoted earlier. Suppose we were able (as in practice we are not) to give a complete specification of the way of life to which we are committed:

> Suppose . . . that we can give it, if the inquirer still goes on asking 'But why *should* I live like that?' then there is no further answer to give him, because we have already *ex hypothesi,* said everything that could be included in this further answer. We can only ask him to make up his own mind which way he ought to live, for in the end everything rests upon such a decision of principle. He has to decide whether to accept that way of life or not; if he accepts it, then we can proceed to justify the decisions that are based upon it; if he does not accept it, then let him accept some other and try to live by it.[13]

[12] *The Language of Morals,* p. 150.
[13] Ibid., p. 69.

This philosophical approach stresses two characteristically romantic themes, sincerity and commitment, although it does so primarily in order to solve a logical problem. If the function of moral language is to guide choices, there must, it seems, be some logical connection between my use of the word 'good' (or other word of moral commendation) and my actually doing, or at least choosing to do, the appropriate action. Thus, it is argued, the fundamental weakness of all objectivist theories is that, if they are correct, a man can become convinced that an action open to him would be right and still say 'so what?' and refuse to do it. In the prescriptivist scheme this cannot happen. For within that scheme it is a matter of definition that a man cannot be using a moral word in its evaluative (as distinct from 'inverted comma') sense unless he thereby commits himself to action of the kind indicated. And whenever he is asked to make a moral judgement about any matter, however remote it may seem to be from immediate action—as in judging a historical or fictitious character—the question before him always is 'Am I prepared, in similar situations to this, to act as my judgement requires that he, being so situated, should act?'

Hence what we normally regard as 'weakness of will' tends in the prescriptivist system to be represented as a sort of insincerity. The individual who does not act in accordance with the moral principles he avows shows by that fact that he is not wholly sincere in his avowal of them; there is an element of *mauvaise foi.*

Creativity, sincerity, freedom, commitment; these, then, are romantic values that are formally incorporated within prescriptivism. Other romantic values are not. The prescriptivist need not value spontaneity or variety of experience or mystery or instinct. He need not, and generally does not, express hostility to 'the scientific world-view'. But he does provide a philosophical rationale for those who choose these values, so long as they choose them consistently and sincerely. For his central doctrine about fact and value licenses such choices and protects them from criticism in the name of morality. For, given the doctrine, the critic has no firmer ground to stand upon than has the romantic humanist himself.

If morality consists in the individual's answer to the question, 'how shall I live?', it is likely that different people will give different answers and that the same individual will give different answers at different times. Not only will one man's morality have no authority for another man, unless he chooses to make it his own, but a man at any given time cannot regard himself as bound by his earlier moral choices, except in so far as he elects to be so bound. And there is, arguably, an element of insincerity, in a man's adhering to past decisions in the face of present spontaneous impulses to the contrary. Hence there is a marked tendency to disintegration in romantic humanism. Add to this the free man's unwillingness to be swayed by tradition or convention and you have the commitment to the Zeitgeist which is a familiar feature of the romantic outlook. As Weightman puts it, 'the fashion of the moment becomes as it were a temporary absolute'.[14] But the idea of creativity exercises an independent influence here and directs attention away from the present to the future. For it is plausible to regard the creative man as the one who anticipates the future; what else could his creativity consist in? To the extent that there remain vestiges of the idea of the perfectibility of man these will reinforce this tendency, as also will a certain contagion from the cumulative progress of science.

These ideas have entered very deeply into the attitudes of the contemporary intellectual and are indeed taken for granted by him. Consider, for example, Mr Oliver Whitley's defence of the BBC policy of giving creative writers their head with the minimum of editorial control:

> The artist is a kind of radar. Ezra Pound called him the antenna of the race. Shelley . . . said that poets are 'the mirrors of the gigantic shadows which futurity casts upon the present' . . . The artist sees things sooner than other people, or further off, or both. . . . The artist probes around the outer edges of acceptance, thereby increasing the range of man's understanding of himself . . . So far from accepting a brief to defend the virtues of the present or the past, he claims freedom, and uses it, to indict the present by proclaiming the future.[15]

The notion that a man should be sincere and creative very easily becomes associated with spontaneity and avoidance of hypocrisy, and so with innocence and freedom from repression.

[14] Weightman, op. cit., p. 15.

[15] In an unpublished lecture on 'Tolerance, or Some Thoughts on some responsibilities in Broadcasting' (1966).

That individual is most distinctive whose impulses are strongest and who restrains them least. So the romantic can maintain with Blake: 'Sooner murder an infant in its cradle than nurse unacted desires'.

It is not a great distance from this to the idea, which so absorbs the modern imagination, of the holy criminal, the man who dares to use his freedom and demonstrate his uninhibited spontaneity by violating the most sacred principles of traditional morality. If he himself suffers along with his victims, this is a witness to his readiness to accept all that life has to offer as well as to do all that it permits. Hence the status of the Marquis de Sade as a romantic hero. There is, of course, nothing in subjectivism itself which positively commits a man to these excesses; there is nothing that requires him to give free rein to his impulses. He is free to opt for an austere and disciplined form of life. He may be gentle and unemphatic, or joyously exuberant.

On the other hand there is nothing, either, to *require* that one impulse be subordinated to another. There is no objective principle which says: 'to be a whole man you must develop a character in which some of your inclinations are systematically restrained' and, this being so, it will not be surprising if those impulses prevail which are 'naturally' stronger or which make the greater appeal to the imagination. There is, in particular, no reason why the principles which the individual chooses to make overriding (which constitute, in the prescriptivist sense, his morality) should coincide at all with those of traditional or conventional morality. The Emperor Heliogabalus (to use an example of Hare's) was so attracted by the colour of blood on grass that he was prepared to kill innocent human beings in order to achieve this aesthetic effect. His 'morality' was of a purely aesthetic kind but it could none the less qualify as a morality in the present sense.[16] Heliogabalus is, perhaps, an example too remote and fantastic to be taken seriously. Listen, instead, to Lionel Trilling's account of the romantic insistence upon 'the sentiment of being':

Through the nineteenth century art has as one of its chief intentions to

[16] The example is given in *Freedom and Reason*, p. 161. As prescriptivism is developed in that book, Heliogabalus can be shown to be inconsistent unless prepared himself to be the victim.

induce in the audience the sentiment of being, to recruit the primitive strength that a highly developed culture has diminished. . . . As the century advances the sentiment of being, of being strong, is increasingly subsumed under the conception of personal authenticity. The work of art is itself authentic by reason of its entire self-definition: it is understood to exist wholly by the laws of its own being, which include the right to embody painful, ignoble, or socially inacceptable subject-matters. Similarly the artist seeks his personal authenticity in his entire autonomousness – his goal is to be as self-defining as the art-object he creates. As for the audience, its expectation is that through its communication with the work of art, which may be resistant, unpleasant, even hostile, it acquires the authenticity of which the object itself is the model and the artist the personal example'.[17]

It is easy to see from Trilling's account how this attitude can get carried over from art into life.

The authority of conscience, on this model, is an authority which the individual sets up within himself. It would not be the authority of conscience if it did not make rules and stick to them consistently, but the content of these rules is not prescribed for it. The Sado-masochist can be a conscientious man, so long as he is consistent in his Sado-masochism; and, if this is so, how should conscience prevent him becoming a Sado-masochist, if he otherwise inclined to be one? And perhaps he is inclined to be one to the extent that he sets the highest value on intensity of feeling and finds that, in his search for ever greater intensity, more ordinary experiences disappoint him. This mood is well expressed by a schoolboy: 'What worries me is the reluctance of people to risk insanity for the sake of experience. We all drown in the end, so why not go for the occasional deep-sea dive? My own hope is that we should all learn to gibber. My main fear is that we shall not listen to each other gibbering.'[18] Morality is nothing, we are inclined to say, if it is not a protection against these excesses, but the morality of romantic humanism has no resources from which it might afford such protection.

To say that morality should be a protection against such excesses is implicitly to appeal to a more traditional conception of morality. And at this stage in our investigation it becomes apparent that two conceptions or morality are current

[17] Trilling, op. cit., pp. 99–100.

[18] *Images of Life*, edd. Robin Richardson and John Chapman, S.C.M. (1973), p. 112.

today and that our present confusion about morality is partly due to this. On the one hand we think of morality as primarily the possession of the individual(though, or course, he may share it with others). It consists of the attitudes and principles he adopts for the ordering of his life and is prepared to recommend others to adopt; which, in the event of conflict, he regards as overriding. The characteristic idiom of this way of thinking is the use of 'morality' in the plural. We have become accustomed to talking of liberal morality or bourgeois morality, the protestant or even the Shakespearean ethic. 'Moralities' represent alternative options between which we are free to choose.

On the other hand we also continue to think and speak of 'morality' in the singular as a set of principles binding upon all men, whose function it is to check the individual's impulses in the interests of others. Only a minority are sophisticated enought to be quite at home with the notion of alternative moralities and even they let go of it sometimes. There is for workaday purposes a moral code which is sufficiently accepted in our society—at least we feel intuitively that there ought to be—and for the unsophisticated most of the time and the sophisticated some of the time, this it what is meant by 'morality'.

The subjectivist gives his own account of this state of affairs. There is, no doubt, a traditional or conventional morality, which (to use Hare's expressive metaphor) has been largely 'incapsulated' in our language. In a society with a Christian past this conventional morality is likely to have been infected with Christian assumptions, and it is not surprising that it should often seem, even now, to be self-evident to many people who are not professing Christians. In just the same way the great Victorian agnostics found it natural to believe that the morality they accepted, which was substantially Christian, stood in no need of supernatural backing. But for the subjectivist this appearance of objectivity is, nevertheless, an illusion. It is for us to exercise our freedom in criticizing this tradtional ethic and in taking over as much or as little of it as we independently decide.

But, we tend to ask, can this account do justice to our obstinate conviction that we are not entirely free to pick and choose among 'moralities' but are compelled to recognize at least *some* moral demands, whether we like them or not? Much of our traditional morality may be a legacy from the Christian centuries, but is this true of all of it? Are there not moral notions which command the allegiance of decent men and women everywhere?

This is a characteristically Anglo-Saxon appeal and the type of humanism I propose to discuss next is a typically (if not quite uniquely) Anglo-Saxon phenomenon. I shall call it 'liberal humanism'. It is best understood as an accommodation or compromise between rational humanism and romantic humanism. It represents, I believe, the moral standpoint of the average English or American intellectual, who is attracted by the libertarian appeal of romantic humanism but cannot stomach its anarchic implications. It is, after all, hard to see how there could exist a *society* of solitary romantics, each legislating in sovereign autonomy for himself and others. Yet it is obvious that no individual can grow to maturity and become a human personality at all, capable of generating his own ideals, except in a society of some kind. Romantic humanism, that is to say, suffers from an ineradicable incoherence, if taken as a complete account of morality.

There must be a basic social framework if the interesting personalities so dear to the romantic are to develop, let alone flourish. To be effective this cannot be at the mercy of individual decision. It must, that is to say, be an objective morality. And in fact the broad outlines of such a morality can be discerned in societies of very diverse cultural and religious backgrounds—as emerges clearly from A. M. Macbeath's study of the anthropological evidence in his Gifford Lectures, *Experiments in Living.*[19] It comprises what C. S. Lewis called 'the ultimate platitudes of practical reason'.

The platitudes do not get much attention because, being platitudes, they are not particularly interesting. They are taken for granted. People who in their everyday life respect them need not be very exciting, or, if they are exciting, it is not this characteristic which makes them so. It is easy, therefore, to overlook their importance; particularly easy, perhaps, for intellectuals who have a connoisseur's interest in what differ-

[19] Macmillan (1952).

entiates people. It is, of course, true that ways of life vary—not only the ways of life that men have, in fact, practised, but the ways of life they have thought worth attempting. The modern mind, with its romantic bias, is entirely alive to the diversity and, in many respects, the incompatibility, of competing ways of life; and its tendency is to emphasize this feature and to neglect, or even to deny, the fundamental platitudes which they have in common. This tendency has been accentuated by the work of anthropologists, some of whom have uncritically assumed that their discipline presupposes a thoroughgoing cultural relativism. The anthropologist is interested primarily in explaining the content of any system of morality in terms of its function in maintaining the way of life of a particular society and everything he says about it is relative to the culture of that society. Within the framework of such an enquiry there is no room, and no need, for comparison between the standards of different societies. This methodological restriction can be uncritically erected into a philosophical principle. Ethical intuitionists, like Sir David Ross, who called attention to the widespread acceptance of the platitudes, were accordingly accused of simply manifesting a preference for the ethical norms of their own society. As A. C. Ewing remarked:

> Ross's *prima facie* duties have most unfairly been described as just the code of the English gentleman. But it would surely be hard to find a community anywhere in which the fact that you had made a promise was not regarded as a reason for keeping it; the fact that you had harmed someone, as a reason for making reparation; the fact that someone had intentionally benefited you, as a reason for showing gratitude. Even such a perverted system as that of the Nazis, did not reject the *prima facie* duties as such, but gave bad reasons for breaking them in a number of cases.[20]

Like earlier rationalists Ross and other intuitionists thought that these prima-facie duties were self-evident. They were known by an intuition akin to that by which, in his view, the axioms of Euclidean geometry were known. We just, so to speak, 'see' that we ought to refrain from murder, keep promises, tell the truth, etc. and there is no further explanation to be given why we have these obligations and not others. They were, that is to say, rational humanists of an old-fashioned

[20] *Second Thoughts in Moral Philosophy*, Routledge & Kegan Paul (1959), p. 40.

kind. It is not surprising that anthropologists, and social scientists generally, were dissatisfied with this position. It is obvious enough that such moral rules have a social function and it is hard to believe that their obligatory character is unrelated to it. As Macbeath points out:

> Any tolerable form of social life requires that there should be rules governing the relations between persons in regard to such matters as intercommunication, return for services rendered, sex relations, respect for life and property etc., and that they should be generally obeyed. And the rules contained in lists of prima facie obligations are in general such obvious conditions of individual and social well-being that most of them are included in the moral codes of most peoples.[21]

Perhaps the most interesting discussion of the matter is to be found in Professor Herbert Hart's *The Concept of Law.* He considers it under the heading, 'The Minimum Content of Natural Law'. What he there discusses is, he admits, 'only a very attenuated version of Natural Law', for the traditional doctrine based natural law on a metaphysical conception of the good for man and, as Hart says, 'Aristotle includes in it the disinterested cultivation of the human intellect, and Aquinas the knowledge of God, and both these represent values which may be and have been challenged.'[22] The truisms which he sets forth (more correctly called 'truisms' than 'platitudes') are based simply on 'the argument that without such a content law and morals could not forward the minimum purpose of survival which men have in associating with each other'.

Hart lists five truisms:

> (1) *Human vulnerability.* . . . If men were to lose their vulnerability to each other there would vanish one obvious reason for the most characteristic provision of law and morals: *Thou shalt not kill.*
>
> (2) *Approximate equality.* . . . This fact of approximate equality, more than other, makes obvious the necessity for a system of mutual forbearance and compromise, which is the base of both legal and moral obligation. [In the absence of such a system life would be, in the Hobbesian phrase, 'solitary, poor, nasty, brutish and short'.] . . .
>
> (3) *Limited altruism.* . . . Men are not devils . . . but neither are they angels; and the fact that they are a mean between these two extremes makes a system of mutual forbearance both necessary and possible. . . .

[21] Op. cit., p. 369.

[22] *The Concept of Law,* Clarendon Press (1961), p. 187.

(4) *Limited resources*. . . . Human beings need food, clothes, and shelter. . . . but [these] are scarce, have to be grown or won from nature, or have to be constructed from human toil. These facts alone make indispensable some minimal form of the institution of property (though not necessarily individual property) and the distinctive kind of rule that requires respect for it. . . .

(5) *Limited understanding and strength of will*. . . . The facts that make rules respecting persons, property and promises necessary in social life are simple and their mutual benefits obvious. Most men are capable of seeing them and of sacrificing the immediate short-term interest which conformity to such rules demands. . . . [But] . . . all are tempted at times to prefer their own immediate interests and, in the absence of a special organization for their detection and punishment, many would succumb to the temptation.[23]

Hart is concerned to draw attention to certain general features of the human situation which render necessary a basic social morality of some kind. He does not in this passage give much indication of the precise content of such a morality, but what matters at this point is less the precise content of such a list of platitudes than the principle upon which it is compiled. The obligations and virtues which occur in the list are there because their recognition and sufficient practice is held to be a necessary condition of any tolerable human existence. They are not logically necessary, as Kant thought, but, to use Strawson's phrase, 'humanly necessary'.

If this scheme is accepted it provides, within certain limits, an objective morality that is capable of rational justification. It concedes at least some of the central claims of rational humanism without seeking the authority of science or appealing to dubious 'intuitions' or problematical conceptions of 'nature', and to that extent restricts the freedom of the romantic humanist to devise a morality which is the unrestrained expression of his own personality. For, should he object to the concept of a basic social morality as such, he could be made to recognize that it is a necessary condition of any social life, which in turn is a necessary condition of his realizing his own purposes, or indeed of his becoming a person at all. If he objected to reciprocity as a feature of morality he could be made to see that a putative moral system which lacked this feature could not perform its function of harmonizing people's interests. If he objected to the inclusion in

[23] Op. cit., pp. 190–3.

a moral system of particular requirements, such as that he should tell the truth or keep promises or condemn cruelty or commend courage, he could be shown that these are necessary features of any system capable of furthering men's interests to the extent needed for a stable society.

But this basic morality is also strictly limited in its range and scope. It falls far short of the developed morality of any civilized society. Insistence upon this limitation is an essential feature of liberal humanism, which seeks to restrict the individual's moral choice only so far as is needed for the bare minimum of social control. The defect of rational humanism in all its forms, and more especially in the form of scientific humanism, is that it bases too much upon too little. It claims to be able, in principle at least, to devise a morality that will satisfy the needs of all men everywhere and to found it upon reason rather narrowly defined. It lacks a sense of the depth and the uniqueness of the individual. Its utilitarian structure turns all decisions into moral decisions, while at the same time depriving them of any personal colouring. Hence the romantic protest in the name of all that it excludes, the passions, the imagination, the urge to personal commitment.

But, as we have seen, romantic protest cannot of itself maintain a continuing culture. It is a fertilizer which, if sparingly applied, can help to produce a rich diversity of flowers from the firm soil of tradition, but which, if used without restriction, must become a solvent of the soil which nourishes it. There must be a basic social structure if the interesting personalities so dear to the romantic are to develop, let alone flourish. This, then, provides the starting-point for liberal humanism.

4

Liberal Humanism

This position (though he does not give it this name) has been worked out with much sensitivity and ingenuity by Sir Peter Strawson in his essay, 'Social Morality and Individual Ideal', and I cannot do better than discuss his formulation of it. Strawson begins by denying what rational humanists characteristically affirm, that all moral claims must have the character of universal principles holding for all men. Morality may be 'not what is demanded of men as men but what is demanded of Spartans by other Spartans or of a King by his subjects'. There are, however, elements in morality that are universal.

What is universally demanded by the members of a moral community is something like the abstract virtue of justice; a man should not insist on a particular claim while refusing to acknowledge any reciprocal claim. But from this formally universal feature of morality no consequences follow as to the universality of application of the particular rules in the observance of which, in particular situations and societies, justice consists.[1]

Beyond this formal requirement there are certain substantial features which must be present in the morality of every society:

It is also important to recognize that certain human interests are so fundamental and so general that they must be universally acknowledged in some form and to some degree in any conceivable moral community.... It remains true that the recognition of certain general virtues and obligations will be a logically or humanly necessary feature of almost any conceivable moral system.[2]

There follows Strawson's version of the platitudes: some form of obligation to mutual aid and mutual abstention from injury and, in some form and in some degree, the virtue of honesty.

But there is a great deal in any developed morality which goes beyond these universal features. Here Strawson makes the move which distinguishes him from the pure rationalist or

[1] *Philosophy* (1961); reprinted in *Christian Ethics and Contemporary Philosophy*, ed. I. T. Ramsey, S.C.M. (1966), p. 291. It is also included in P. F. Strawson, *Freedom and Resentment*, Methuen (1974).

[2] Op. cit., pp. 291 f.

romantic. There is, he says, a distinction to be made between the sphere of morality and the region of the ethical. The sphere of morality has to do with the observance of such rules as are necessary for the existence of a society, which in turn is a necessary condition of the realization of any human ideals. Within this sphere, and within this sphere only, rational procedures can discover truth in matters of morality. The region of the ethical, by contrast, is 'a region in which there are truths which are incompatible with one another'. Strawson introduces this conception as follows:

> Men make for themselves pictures of ideal forms of life. Such pictures are various, and may be in sharp opposition to each other; and one and the same individual may be captivated by different and sharply conflicting pictures at different times. At one time it may seem to him that he should live – even that *a man* should live – in such and such a way; at another that the only truly satisfactory form of life is something totally different, incompatible with the first. In this way his outlook may vary radically not only at different periods of his life, but from day to day, even from one hour to the next.[3]

Related to these individual ideals are 'profound truths' about man and the universe:

> There exist, that is to say, many profound general statements which are capable of capturing the ethical imagination in the same way . . . They often take the form of general descriptive statements about man and the world. They can be incorporated into a metaphysical system, or dramatized in a religious or historical myth. Or they can exist – their most persuasive form for many – as isolated statements such as, in France, there is a whole literature of, the literature of the maxim. I will not give examples, but I will mention names. One cannot read Pascal or Flaubert, Nietzsche or Goethe, Shakespeare or Tolstoy, without encountering these profound truths. It is certainly possible, in a coolly analytical frame of mind, to mock at the whole notion of the profound truth; but we are guilty of mildly bad faith if we do. For in most of us the ethical imagination succumbs again and again to *these* pictures of man, and it is precisely as truths that we wish to characterize them while they hold us captive.[4]

The 'pictures of ideal forms of life' and the 'profound truths about man and the universe' reflect one another and capture the imagination in the same way:

> Hence it is as wholly futile to think that we could, without destroying their character, systematize these truths into one coherent body of truth

[3] Op. cit., p. 280.

[4] Op. cit., pp. 282 f.

as it is to suppose that we could, without destroying their character, form a coherent composite image from these images. This may be expressed by saying that the region of the ethical is the region where there are truths but no truth; or, in other words, that the injunction to see life steadily *and* see it whole is absurd, for one cannot do both.[5]

I think it is fair to say that Strawson here shows himself to be fundamentally a romantic who makes minimal concessions to the practically unavoidable claims of organized society. The basic notion is that we have, so to speak, an agreed moral syllabus, which is reasonable and can be shown to be reasonable. Beyond that we are offered a range of optional further subjects. What makes life interesting and exciting is the optional further subjects, but the agreed syllabus is essential, because the moral rules it enjoins and the moral virtues it encourages are the necessary conditions of any tolerable human life, *a fortiori* of the successful achievement by anyone of his own individual ideal or ideals.

Strawson's commitment to the romantic ideal is apparent in his appreciation of 'evaluative diversity'. Having asserted that 'the region of the ethical . . . is a region in which many . . . incompatible pictures may secure the imaginative, though doubtless not often the practical allegiance of a single person' he continues:

Moreover this statement itself may be seen not merely as a description of what is the case, but as a positive evaluation of evaluative diversity. Any diminution of this variety would impoverish the human scene. The multiplicity of conflicting pictures is itself the essential element in one of one's pictures of man.[6]

It is this which justifies my use of the title 'liberal humanism' to characterize this particular standpoint. Strawson himself gives eloquent expression to his vision of a liberal society:

What will be the attitude of one who experiences sympathy with a variety of conflicting ideals of life? It seems that he will be most at home in a liberal society, in a society in which there are variant moral environments but in which no ideal endeavours to engross, and determine the character of the common morality. He will not argue in favour of such a society that it gives the best chance for the truth about life to prevail. Nor will he argue in its favour that it has the best chance of producing a harmonious kingdom of ends, for he will not think of ends as

[5] Op. cit., p. 283.

[6] Ibid.

necessarily capable of being harmonized. He will simply welcome the ethical diversity which the society makes possible, and in proportion as he values that diversity he will note that he is the natural, though perhaps the sympathetic, enemy of all those whose single intense vision of the ends of life drives them to try to make the requirements of the ideal co-extensive with those of common social morality.[7]

This is not the classical case for liberalism, as Strawson clearly recognizes. As set out by Milton and Kant and J. S. Mill, that case was that the greatest practical enlargement of the area of personal freedom is an indispensable means to the discovery of the truth about life and so to the attainment of happiness; it being assumed that the truth about life could, in principle, be ascertained and that men can agree in recognizing happiness when they see it. Classical liberalism was founded on a thoroughly objectivist moral philosophy.

The new style of liberalism is familiar to us as the philosophy underlying the 'permissive society'. It finds expression in a great deal of what one reads in, say, the *Guardian* or the *Observer,* or hears on the BBC. Professor H. L. A. Hart in his *Law, Liberty, and Morality*[8] provides a clear and confident statement of it in relation to jurisprudence; and it is interesting to notice that Hare in *Freedom and Reason* develops his earlier views in a direction that brings them very much closer to Strawson's.[9] Here too there is a broad division between the region of the strictly moral and the realm of ideals. Critics of Hare's earlier work had complained that it presented no limits to the possible content of moral principles–Heliogabalus, if prepared to be consistent, was as much a moralist as Socrates, though a more eccentric one; and that it allowed no rational means of choosing between rival moral theories–between Socrates and Heliogabalus. Hare in the later book argues that, in a situation where another's interests are affected, a man can always be pressed to say what action he would be prepared to recommend, if the roles were reversed. Thus a Nazi would be required to decide whether he would recommend that, if he were a Jew, he should be gassed. Since he does not himself wish to be gassed, he cannot sincerely recommend this and is, therefore, committed to moral condemnation of the practice

[7] Op. cit., pp. 297 f.

[8] Oxford University Press, 1968.

[9] He acknowledges the affinity in *Freedom and Reason,* pp. 151–2.

of gassing Jews. These 'golden-rule arguments' result from combining his earlier requirements of prescriptivity and universalizability with the actual inclinations of the agent. From this sort of argument Hare envisages two 'respectable' ways out, as well as a number of less respectable ways. One of the respectable ways is an appeal to utilitarian considerations. If the Nazi were able to show that it was in the general interest (when equal weight has been given to the interests of each individual) that Jews should be gassed, then he could justify the gassing of Jews, even though he himself, if a Jew, would not wish to be gassed. The other respectable way is for the Nazi to adopt the extermination of the Jews as an ideal to which he is ready, if need be, to sacrifice people's interests, *including his own.* A man who is prepared in this way to subordinate interests to ideals Hare calls a 'fanatic'. The fanatic puts himself beyond moral argument; but, fortunately human nature is so constituted that fanatics are few. Or so Hare believes.

But not only fanatics have ideals. What makes a man a fanatic is not his having ideals, but his being prepared to sacrifice interests to ideals. There are, Hare believes, two distinct grounds for moral condemnation or commendation, interests and ideals of human excellence; and, although tempting, it will not do to limit morality entirely to the former. 'Golden-rule arguments' are applicable only where interests are affected, but there are moral questions which are not concerned with interests. Hare instances the case of a pretty girl who earns her living by strip-tease: 'Those who call such exhibitions immoral do not do so because of their effect on other people's interests; for, since everbody gets what he or she wants, nobody's interests are harmed. They are likely, rather, to use such words as "degrading"'.[10] Hare does not, therefore, restrict the use of the term 'moral' to the cases where interests are affected, but his difference from Strawson on this point is verbal only. Both distinguish between ideals, on the one hand, and, on the other, a sort of morality based on people's interests. They do not give the same account of this sort of morality, though Strawson's emphasis upon reciprocity matches what Hare has to say about golden-rule arguments. Where they

[10] Op. cit., p. 147.

appear to differ is about the justification of the sort of morality based on interests. Strawson finds it in the fact that morality of this sort is a necessary condition of the existence of any tolerable society; Hare is content to base it on the formal properties of moral arguments taken in conjunction with the actual inclinations of individuals. Thus all moral arguments are for him *ad hominem* as they are not for Strawson—although Hare would claim that the appearance of arbitrariness is mitigated by the *de facto* similarity of people's basic inclinations.

Liberal humanism is now the very air we breathe. For this reason, and because of its all-embracing tolerance, we find it hard to notice its premisses or to find fault with them, if we do. Are not all rival ideologies given their due? Are they not indeed encouraged, subject only to a basic social morality whose necessity all reasonable men can recognize? The strength of its appeal lies in its claim to provide an entirely non-controversial system of morality which satisfies the requirement for an effective method of social control, while allowing as much scope as they can reasonably expect for the proponents of other, less hospitable, moralities. The question is whether these claims can be made good.

It is significant that Strawson does not draw any very clear distinction between 'individual ideals' and 'profound general statements about man and the universe'. Yet they are very different. Christianity and Marxism are obvious examples of 'profound general statements about man and the universe'. Here, by contrast, is Strawson's list of typical 'ideal pictures of life':

> The ideal of self-obliterating devotion to duty or to the service of others;
> of personal honour and magnanimity;
> of asceticism, contemplation, retreat;
> of action, dominance and power;
> of the cultivation of an 'exquisite sense of the luxurious':
> of simply human solidarity and cooperative endeavour;
> of a refined complexity of social existence;
> of a constantly maintained and renewed affinity with natural things;[11]

Any of these, he says, 'may form the core and substance of a personal ideal'. And later he mentions as an ideal picture of

[11] Op. cit., p. 280.

life 'that in which the command to love one another becomes the supreme value'. Ideals then, are *prescriptive*; they tell us how to live; the 'profound general statements' are *descriptive*; they offer an over-all interpretation of the human condition.

Not only are Strawson's 'individual ideals' plainly in a different category from his 'profound general statements'; they differ markedly in kind from one another. The ideal of self-obliterating devotion to duty and of service to others, and the ideal of loving one another are both, recognizably, answers to the question, how *a man* should live. One could scarcely embrace them merely as a personal preference, still less as a transitory one. The remainder one could embrace without in any way regarding them as incumbent upon other people. They are answers, rather, to the question, how shall *I* live? The ideals which (to use Strawson's expression) 'reflect and are reflected by' profound general statements about men and the universe are, characteristically, of the first kind: answers to the question how *a man* should live; and they vary precisely because they reflect different conceptions of what it is to be a man. The others are essentially vocational. They represent the individual's sense of what he has it in him to be or do in virtue of his individual temperament or endowment. It is one of the merits of Strawson's discussion—one which it shares with romanticism—that he notices these vocational ideals, which moral philosophers are inclined to neglect. But not all ideals are in this way personal and vocational; some are general ideals of human excellence. And these latter are intimately associated with a man's entire philosophy of life, upon which depends his conception of what it is to be a man, and what is the significance of human life.

The relation between such ideals of human excellence and the corresponding philosophies of life—Strawson's 'profound general statements'—is exemplified in Strawson's scheme. Strawson has his own 'individual ideal' which I think we may take as more than just a vocational one. It is the ideal of imaginative sympathy with the ideals of others, no matter how alien these may be. It reflects a view of man as a being who, within the limits of his biological constitution, is free to become what he wills, whose 'existence precedes his essence'. If men are self-creations of this sort and if, as Strawson believes, there are no objective criteria by which to judge what they choose to make of themselves, one can help them, once their basic needs are satisfied, only by identifying oneself in imagination with their entire project of life, or their changing projects, and aiding their achievement; so long, that is, as they respect the basic social morality. It is characteristic of a being, such as man is on this view, that he expresses himself, among other ways, in the elaboration of religious and metaphysical systems which he is tempted to regard as true; and Strawson will sympathize with these, while recognizing this temptation for what it is, a delusive phantasy.

So Strawson presents us with an ideal picture of life based upon a profound general statement about man and the universe, which, on his own theory, we are at liberty to accept or reject as we choose, for it falls within the region of the ethical.

As soon as this has become apparent, it is clear that Strawson's scheme, for all its air of benevolent neutrality, cannot satisfy those who are serious adherents of any alternative ideology or philosophy of life. Neither the Christian nor the Marxist, for example, can agree that his Christianity or his Marxism should occupy the status merely of a private preference with no authority over man's social life and no claim to objective truth. Christianity and Marxism are not 'personal ideals' or 'profound statements' which can fit happily into the niche that the liberal humanist is ready to provide for them; they are rival philosophies of life.

Not only the Christian or the Marxist but the scientific humanist also will decline the role he is offered, because he believes that man is a rational animal to meet whose needs, when they are properly and scientifically understood, a reasonable morality can be devised. He will, if he is sensible, recognize that there are ideals of a purely personal, vocational kind; but he has his own universal ideal of an objective, scientifically based morality, which can be shown to be reasonable to anyone not influenced by traditional prejudice or suffering from psychological immaturity. This scientifically based 'picture of man', just because it is scientifically based, he is unwilling to regard as a matter for purely personal choice, as one among a number of incompatible 'truths'.

The liberal humanist, faced by this challenge, may perhaps

agree that he is not conceding to his rivals all that they wish to claim, but argue nevertheless that he grants them all that they can reasonably ask. There is a minimum social morality which can be rationally defended, based on human needs that are so fundamental and inescapable that they cannot be gainsaid; but, he will insist, it falls far short of what the scientific humanist believes he can establish, much of which cannot be derived from science or, indeed, arrived at by any other rational process. It falls within the region of the ethical, not the sphere of the moral. And the same, *mutatis mutandis,* is true of the others. The fundamental question, however, is whether this crucial distinction between the moral and the ethical can be maintained; and whether, if it can, it is as exhaustive and exclusive as Strawson makes out. Because of it he has to introduce a radical discontinuity into his account of the good life. He has to say that there are certain virtues such as honesty and (with certain qualifications), justice, which belong to the minimum social morality; these are firmly based in the nature of man as a social being and are, therefore, part of the agreed moral syllabus. There are other virtues, such as humility and chastity, which are optional subjects and are based only on pictures of human nature, which men are free to adopt or not as they choose. There are, it would seem, conclusive arguments in favour of honesty. There are no arguments at all in favour of chastity, only choices. A similar discontinuity is observable in Hare's *Freedom and Reason,* where ideals of human excellence are sharply distinguished from interests, so that we are not permitted to argue in the case of the stripper, that it is not in the girl's interest to accept degrading employment, just because it is degrading.[12]

This discontinuity is extremely implausible. What makes it attractive is the hope it offers of providing a basic morality which is as modest in its pretensions as it is unchallengeable in its demands. The sharpness of the contrast between it and the realm of ideals is essential to the scheme, for it is this that prevents the basic morality becoming infected with

[12] This is because 'interest' is defined in terms of wants. 'To have an interest is, crudely speaking, for there to be something which one wants, or is likely in the future to want, or which is (or is likely to be) a means necessary or sufficient for the attainment of something which one wants (or is likely to want)' (*Freedom and Reason,* p.122).

ideals or ideals claiming the categorical character of the basic morality.

But it is open to a serious objection. The 'agreed syllabus' does not and, I suggest, could not constitute the entire morality of any actual society; for beyond the minimum moral content which is 'humanly necessary', it provides only an abstract scheme into which some content has to be poured. Take, for example, sexual morality. Although there are wide variations between societies in respect of the sexual codes they have recognized, there is no society which has regarded sexual behaviour as of no social concern; and this is not surprising since sexual desire is universal, fundamental, and extremely exigent. Our own society has until recently based itself on a Christian ideal which limits sexual intercourse to marriage and regards marriage as a life-long partnership between a man and a woman. In spite of recent erosion this conception is still deeply embedded in our legal system and affects the related institutions of property and parenthood. This sexual morality with all its social ramifications is, of course, only one of the possible ways of organizing a 'system of reciprocal demands' having to do with sex. There can be no doubt that the desires for sexual intercourse and parenthood are among the human interests which are 'so fundamental that they must be universally acknowledged in some form and in some degree in any conceivable moral community'. The question is, for a given society, in what form and in what degree. It is not at all clear how Strawson would answer this question. He will, of course, admit that the question could be answered (as in our society it has been so far) by reference to a particular ideal form of life which has been the focus of aspiration for the members of society, giving its sanction to the mutual obligations of husbands and wives, parents and children; encouraging and, in turn, depending upon such virtues as fidelity and chastity. But this is to 'make the requirements of the ideal coextensive with those of the common social morality', which he is against. Is he, perhaps, prepared to argue (as Comfort, Osborn, and other rational humanists would) that a rational choice can be made between alternative patterns of sexual ethics in terms of the human satisfaction they offer? But to admit this possibility is to abandon the characterization of ideal forms of life as reflecting 'truths which are incompatible with one another'.

Precisely the same point could be made about the institution of property. Some form of the institution is necessary to any stable society—this much is a platitude—but it has to be some determinate form and the basic social morality does not lay down which this is to be. And in this case, too, whatever form of the institution is adopted encourages and depends upon the appropriate moral virtues. There is thus a vast area intermediate between Strawson's sphere of the moral and region of the ethical which is of enormous social importance, but which the liberal humanist typically neglects. It also directly affects the individual and his vocational ideals to the extent that these are related to the social roles that he discharges. If he decides that by talent and temperament he is called to be a doctor or a lawyer or a scholar he is committed by that choice to the ethic of his chosen profession, which he may be able to influence to some degree but cannot vary at will. The tendency of liberal humanism with its strong romantic strain, is to weaken the authority of all such institutional claims upon the individual, which come to be regarded as a vast impersonal system threatening his creative freedom of expression. And this attitude reinforces the atomizing tendencies that are already at work in our society, so as to make it increasingly resemble this picture. Thus genuine community is doubly threatened; first by the determination of the tough-minded to eliminate all that is merely customary or in any way anomalous; second by the reluctance of the tender-minded to countenance any institutional loyalties. For illustration we need look no further than the universities whose way of life is under constant pressure both from those who think in terms of the minimum university and talk of 'efficient use of the plant' and 'pupil contact hours', and from those whose idea of a community is a temporary huddle of like-minded individuals bound by no institutional ties. The liberal humanist may reply that there *is* an ideal which should inform our moral system, viz. the one Strawson himself favours, that of imaginative sympathy with the ideals of others. But this is a second-order ideal which can qualify a moral system only, so to speak, adverbially. Given that in the society certain virtues are acknowledged and certain obligations recognized, the members of it can be tolerant and sympathetic in their judgement upon those who, for whatever reason, are at odds with the standards set; but tolerance and sympathy do not of themselves generate a system of moral demands, since their essence is to be morally permissive.

Faced then by the distinction which the liberal humanist draws between ideals that are not amenable to rational choice and a basic social morality that can be shown to be 'humanly necessary', and his insistence that the two be kept apart, we have to insist that his programme cannot be carried through as it stands. We have no alternative but to make, as a society, certain moral decisions which presuppose some ideal of human excellence and cannot be determined solely by the minimum basic morality. The attempted accommodation between rational and romantic humanism, to be achieved by parcelling out the territory between them, breaks down. Either the region of ideals must be opened up to rational argument or the sphere of the moral must be allowed to admit of controversy.

As it happens both alternatives seem, on reflection, to be demanded. More argument is possible about ideals than Strawson is prepared to admit and the basic morality is more controversial than he supposes. A man's view, Strawson tells us, may vary from day to day, even from hour to hour, as to what is the only truly satisfactory form of life; and so of course, it may. But, if a picture of life presents itself as the only truly satisfactory one, the question seems to arise, at the least, whether it is *a* satisfactory one. Quite simply, does it satisfy? Or would it satisfy if persevered with? Can one reasonably allow oneself to be captivated by attractive images of possible lives without raising the question whether or not their appeal is delusive? In day dreams, of course, we can do this. If, however, we are not day-dreaming, but seriously considering the question how we ought to live we must, at the very least, take notice of certain undeniable needs and inescapable facts; we must, that is, if we are trying to be reasonable; psychologically speaking we can, no doubt, avoid taking notice of them by retreating into madness or simple silliness. A picture of human life which took no account of hunger or thirst or sexual desire or the need for shelter and companionship or the inevitability of death, would not be a serious picture of human life at all.

There are pictures of human life which exist in the realm of fantasy, the world of the fairy-tale, where wishes always come true and people live happily ever after, and the weak overcome the strong and good is never worsted by evil. Such pictures may fulfil a necessary function, but we are rarely tempted to think of them as true, let alone profoundly true. Serious religious or metaphysical schemes would normally be contrasted with such fanciful pictures, and it is reckoned a fatal flaw in them if they cannot do justice to the observed facts of human life or the accepted findings of the sciences. That is to say, they present themselves, and are normally regarded, as candidates for truth.

Moreover it is hard to see how in the end 'profound truths' can be a serious matter if questions of truth or falsehood do not arise in connection with them. Yet, in Strawson's view, they are a serious matter, since they are the intellectual counterparts of those ideals, freedom to choose which is the essential feature of any comprehensive way of life which he is prepared to acknowledge. To choose, then, is important. But how are we to choose? Not, *ex hypothesi,* in terms of truth or evidence. How, then, is a man to decide whether to be a Christian or a Marxist or a liberally minded humanist?

As to the basic morality, Strawson himself recognizes that justice involves only a formal requirement of reciprocity, and this formal requirement may be exemplified by widely differing social systems. The differences are to be accounted for, presumably, by, *inter alia,* the varying ideals that have inspired them. The 'social justice', for example, which has been so influential a conception in post-war British politics, is far from platitudinous and derives from a vision of society which is emphatically repudiated by liberal theorists such as Friedman and Hayek. But other platitudinous virtues are also to some extent open to divergent interpretations. Honesty is universally prized, but there are wide differences of opinion (and even wider differences in practice) as to what honesty requires and to whom it is due. Does it demand for example, the literal truth about the details of a person's earnings to the tax authorities? There are many, and in some countries undoubtedly a majority, who would not think it 'dishonest' to conceal or disguise the truth about such matters. Moreover priorities may differ. Small agricultural communities tend to rate politeness more highly and honesty less highly than complex industrial societies. Hence that endearing, and infuriating, tendency to tell the stranger what it is thought that he would like to hear, rather than the unwelcome truth, about such matters as the time of buses or the distance to the next village. Presumably in a small community most people know what is going on anyway, so mere information is relatively unimportant, whereas avoiding friction matters a great deal.

Moreover the platitudes, although always regarded as important, are not always taken to be of overriding importance, and cultures and individuals differ as to what other values can override them and in what circumstances. As Ewing remarks, 'Even such a perverted system as that of the Nazis did not reject the prima-facie duties as such, but gave (bad) reasons for breaking them in a great number of cases.' Acceptance of the platitudes will not of itself guarantee wise judgement as when they may be overridden. An ethic need not be obviously perverted to illustrate this point. We need only recollect the relative importance attached in aristocratic societies to the preservation of life and the maintenance of personal honour, or, in our own society, to the prevention of injury and convenience in transport. Thus, although the platitudes can never be entirely discounted, their force and scope and relevance is always to some extent limited by the operation of other, non-platitudinous, ideals.

But there is a further consideration which affects the justification of the platitudes. A society, even a complex one, can get along with a degree of honesty or respect for human life which goes little, if at all, beyond what simple prudence would dictate. 'There are certain rules of conduct' says Hart 'which any social organization must maintain if it is to be viable.' But when is an organization 'viable'? If to be viable is just to survive, any surviving society must by this criterion be morally satisfactory. But how can this be seriously maintained in face of the discrimination that has characterized so many societies? A community may deny the most basic rights, as Hart himself has pointed out, not only to members of other communities, but also to some of its own members. And yet, like ancient

Sparta or the Hindu caste system, it may survive for centuries.

If such a community is to be open to criticism on moral grounds, it will have to be not because it neglects the conditions of its survival, but because it neglects the fundamental interests of its members. This is an intuitively far more satisfying criterion, and there is some warrant for it in Strawson's formulation. But, if this criterion is adopted, the basic morality loses much of its claim to be entirely non-controversial. The liberal humanist is confronted, in the end, with a dilemma. Either he bases his minimum social morality upon the necessary conditions for the survival of a society; in which case it is secured from controversy, but only in so far as it is stated in a very general form, which will require further specification in any given society; or he bases it upon a determinate conception of fundamental human needs which is open to some degree of controversy and liable to be influenced by ideals of human excellence.

The liberal humanist may, however, seek to resist this conclusion. He may concede that a society cannot survive on the basic morality alone and that there must be some recourse to ideals if morality is to fulfil its social function, but he may recommend as a remedy what Hart calls 'moral pluralism'. This involves 'divergent sub-moralities in relation to the same area of conduct'.[13] Personal ideals could thus be allowed a social dimension by the encouragement of variant communities within the larger society, each complementing or specifying the basic social morality in its own way in accordance with its distinctive way of life. In addition to the agreed syllabus a selection of further subjects would be required of all candidates, but not the same selection. Should it be found necessary to have some shared values over and above the basic minimum, these could be arrived at by negotiation and compromise.

There is no need to deny that such pluralism represents a possible option, which a society may reasonably endeavour to put into effect. In order to adopt it decisions will have to be taken at a social and political level as to the over-all pattern of life in that society, decisions which are not dictated by the

[13] 'Social Solidarity and the Enforement of Morality', *University of Chicago Law Review*, xxxv (1967). Strawson's recognition that many ideals require a social dimension indicates that he favours 'moral pluralism' of this kind.

basic social morality and belong therefore to Strawson's region of the ethical'. As such they are not, on his view, open to rational debate.

But, as soon as this option is stated, it becomes apparent that there are serious *arguments* available for and against it, in which appeal is made to both practical and broadly moral considerations. People are likely to be less frustrated and readier to accept essential constraints if in important aspects of their lives they are free to do as they wish with others who are like-minded; and, as Mill so strongly believed, such an arrangement allows diverse styles of life to be developed and tested within an over-all framework that is secure and tolerant. There is a case, along these lines, for allowing a variety of forms of marriage or other sexual relationship to be regarded as morally, and perhaps even legally, acceptable. But there are also likely to be severe disadvantages. If any ideal is to have a social dimension, it requires to be supported to some extent by the ethos of society at large. For example the prevalence of divorce as a readily available and socially accepted remedy is bound to weaken the recognition and practice of marriage as a life-long covenant. To avoid this consequence in a thoroughly plural society those who wished to adhere to the latter ideal as one 'option' among others could well be forced eventually to insulate themselves from the rest of society in order to resist the contagion. And this tendency could militate against the mutual confidence and easy social relationships which might otherwise obtain between members of the wider society, while at the same time increasing for the individual that very burden of conformity from which the liberal hoped to free him.

The liberal humanist might well think the price worth paying for greater diversity in sexual relationships. But would he, in the case of property? Here views differ not only as to whether, and to what extent, the institution of private property should be maintained at all, but also as to how far the accumulation and protection of property should be regulated by the state. Almost all societies have been inegalitarian and, in our own society, it is a highly controversial question whether, e.g., it is just to use the state's powers of taxation to secure greater economic and social equality. Both those who favour this and those who object to what they see as 'penal taxation' take their stand upon considerations of justice; and dispute between them defies adjudication by appeal to purely formal tests. There are obvious practical difficulties in adopting a pluralist policy about such matters, and where it has been attempted, as in the United States, there has been continuous pressure toward uniformity. But more important than these practical considerations is the unwillingness of those who adhere seriously to an ideal to allow it to be compromised beyond a certain point. There are limits to what they will tolerate in the way of 'divergent sub-moralities' and in the extent to which they are prepared to sacrifice their own ideal in the attempt to arrive at a general consensus. The most striking contemporary examples are political. Few, however liberal, would be willing to countenance a sub-morality which denied fundamental human rights, notwithstanding the prevalence of world-views that challenge our conception of such rights, or to tolerate customs among tribal minorities which involve the exploitation of women or the religious indoctrination of children. And even in the sexual realm similar lines are drawn in relation to paedophilia or child marriages.[14]

It seems, then, that resort to pluralism does not enable the liberal humanist to avoid the fundamental criticism that his initial distinction between a (rational) basic social morality and (non-rational) individual ideals is untenable. Most of the major decisions which have to be made about our social and political arrangements, even if we opt for pluralism, have to do with ideals, but are at the same time open to rational debate. Ideals are not, as a rule, arbitrarily chosen but depend upon deeply held and broadly ramified convictions about human nature and the human predicament. It is for this reason that, as Mackie remarks: '. . . it is not possible genuinely to adhere to an ideal and at the same time to subordinate it completely to some resultant of all ideals.'[15]

[14] I have discussed this question of 'pluralism' in greater detail in 'Law and the Protection of Institutions' in *The Proper Study,* ed. Vesey, Macmillan (1971).

[15] *Ethics,* p. 154.

5

Two Secular Critics of Humanist Ethics

The three forms of secular humanism that I have discussed so far turn out to be in various ways inadequate, and it is tempting to proceed at once to a consideration of the difference which religion might make, if brought into the discussion. But such a move would be premature. For, although the varieties of humanism I have been considering are extremely influential, it would be arbitrary and unfair to suppose that their weaknesses are apparent only to the religious mind and that they represent the only options open to the secular moralist. And it happens that quite recently these prevailing trends have been subjected to searching criticism by two thinkers whose own position is explicitly non-theistic, Iris Murdoch and Stuart Hampshire.

Iris Murdoch in her book, *The Sovereignty of Good,* directs her attack for the most part upon what I have called 'romantic humanism'; Stuart Hampshire's target in his Leslie Stephen Lecture, *Morality and Pessimism,* is, rather, rational humanism in its philosophical guise, utilitarianism; but they share a certain nostalgia for older, more traditional conceptions of morality.

Iris Murdoch finds in Kant the typical portrait of modern man or 'man-god': for Kant abolished God and made man God in his stead:

> How recognizable, how familiar to us, is the man so beautifully portrayed in the *Grundlegung,* who confronted even with Christ turns away to consider the judgement of his own conscience and to hear the voice of his own reason. Stripped of the exiguous metaphysical background which Kant was prepared to allow him, this man is with us still, free, independent, lonely, powerful, rational, responsible, brave, the hero of so many novels and books of moral philosophy . . . It is not such a very long step from Kant to Nietzsche, and from Nietzsche to existentialism and the Anglo-Saxon ethical doctrines which in some ways closely resemble it. In fact Kant's man had already received a glorious incarnation nearly a century earlier in the work of Milton: his proper name is Lucifer.[1]

[1] *The Sovereignty of Good,* Routledge & Kegan Paul (1970), p. 80.

The characteristic doctrine of morality associated with this man is that of will as the creator of value. 'The agent, thin as a needle, appears in the quick flash of the choosing will.'[2] The idea of good remains indefinable and empty so that human choice may fill it. The world is value-neutral. There is no mystery in it, and agreement about it can be reached in principle by any who are willing to attend to the facts. One is reminded of an operations room with an enormous map covering the whole of one wall and senior officers sticking flags on it, to all appearance arbitrarily. A man's flag-sticking policy is his way of life and, so long as he achieves consistency, it cannot be faulted.

The assumption seems to be, so Iris Murdoch complains, that it is an easy matter to come to see the world as it is; the only difficulty is to decide how to act in it. But this is not so:

It is a *task* to come to see the world as it is. A philosophy which leaves duty without a context and exalts the idea of freedom and power as a separate top level value ignores this task and obscures the relation between virtue and reality. We act rightly 'when the time comes' not out of strength of will but out of the quality of our usual attachments and with the kind of energy and discernment which we have available. And to this the whole activity of our consciousness is relevant.[3]

What chiefly hinders us in this task of seeing the world as it is, she believes, is our concern with 'the fat relentless ego', which involves us in consolatory fantasies. So there is need of a technique which will purify our selfish wills and enable us to act well.

For the religious prayer is such a technique and what is needed is, in effect, a secular analogue of prayer. Like prayer it must be directed towards something transcendent. If this is not God, it must be the idea of goodness itself which, like God, may be thought of as 'a single perfect transcendent non-representable and necessarily real object of attention'.[4] The idea of goodness involves the idea of a standard of perfection, hard to attain, all but impossible to represent, which nevertheless unifies the moral world:

The idea of perfection moves, and possibly changes, us . . . because it inspires love in the part of us that is most worthy . . . It lies always beyond, and it is from this beyond that it exercizes its *authority* . . .

[2] Op. cit., p. 53. [3] Op. cit., pp. 91–2. [4] Op. cit., p. 55.

Beyond the details of craft and criticism there is only the magnetic non-representable idea of the good which remains not 'empty' so much as mysterious.[5]

Miss Murdoch is fully aware that in this account of goodness she is drawing upon both Christian and Platonic sources. She wants above all to retain what these have in common, the sense of goodness as a transcendent demand which has authority over the individual will and is in no sense its creation. But she is equally decisive in her rejection of Christian and Platonic metaphysics, although in neither case does she make the grounds of her rejection at all explicit. She is content to assert, as against Plato, that:

The Good has nothing to do with purpose, indeed it excludes the idea of purpose. 'All is vanity' is the beginning and end of ethics. The only genuine way to be good is to be good 'for nothing' in the midst of a scene where every 'natural' thing, including one's own mind, is subject to chance, that is, to necessity.[6]

and, as against theism, that 'almost everything that consoles us is a fake . . . In the case of the idea of a transcendent personal God the degeneration of the idea seems scarcely avoidable.'[7] Hence it is appropriate to reflect upon Miss Murdoch's essay as a critique of romantic humanism from within an entirely secular standpoint and as an attempt to provide a more adequate basis for a secular ethic.

The two features of the modern outlook to which she takes exception are the fragmentation of the self, which brings about the decay of the ideas of virtue and vice as permanent dispositions of the soul; and the vision of the world as metaphysically neutral and readily open to casual inspection and consequent agreement.

How might 'modern man' be expected to reply? He would, in the first instance, I think, point out that her vision of the world is the same as his in all respects save one, and that one highly problematic. For she believes, as he does, that:

Human life has no external point or *telos* . . . There are properly many patterns or purposes within life, but there is no general and as it were generally guaranteed pattern or purpose of the kind for which philosophers and theologians used to search. We are what we seem to be, transient, mortal creatures, subject to necessity and chance.[8]

[5] Op. cit., p. 62. [6] Op. cit., p. 71. [7] Op. cit., p. 59. [8] Op. cit., p. 79.

It seems to follow that she has no quarrel with 'the scientific world-view' in its less grandiose forms, for all *it* does is to document the doctrine that the world is ruled by chance and necessity. How then, modern man could ask, is morality to be conceived in such a world? Either it must be based on science; or it must be a construction of the human mind exercising its own creative autonomy; or it must be some compromise between these two. Yet Miss Murdoch is critical of all three options. Although the main thrust of her attack is against the romantic pretensions of post-Kantian man, she is equally opposed to any form of utilitarianism, for this is involved in her insistence on 'the pointlessness of virtue and its unique value and the endless extent of its demand'.[9] *A fortiori* she could not be content with any accommodation between the two.

Iris Murdoch would protest against the implication that there are no other possibilities. It is the whole burden of her essay that there is a transcendent good in the light of which we can see things as they really are when the preoccupations of the self are laid aside as they are characteristically in the creation and contemplation of great works of art. To look properly at evil and human suffering is almost insuperably difficult, but:

> There is, however, something in the serious attempt to look compassionately at human things which automatically suggests that 'there is more than this'. The 'there is more than this', if it is not to be corrupted by some sort of quasi-theological finality, must remain a very tiny spark of insight, something with, as it were, a metaphysical position, but no metaphysical form. But it seems to me that the spark is real, and that great art is evidence of its reality.[10]

What can scarcely fail to strike the reader about Miss Murdoch's treatment of her theme is the absence, surprising in a novelist, of all discussion of the particular case, all attempt at illustration. We are not even given examples of the sort of great art to which she attributes such crucial moral significance nor of how it achieves its effects. Nor even, at a theoretical level, are we provided with an account of what is involved in seeing the world as it is or why it should be so difficult. However, what is here missing is to be found in two of her earlier works,

[9] Op. cit., p. 104.

[10] Op. cit., p. 73.

'Vision and Choice in Morality'[11] and her monograph on *Sartre*.[12] In the former she argues, as it seems to me with great persuasiveness, that the separation of fact and value upon which philosophers have so strongly insisted is not a logical requirement of any meta-ethics, but a contingent feature of a particular, liberal, moral outlook. Every morality reflects a characteristic 'vision of the world', and the account of morality offered by the prescriptivist represents one such vision. The philosopher who claims that a man's morality is constituted by the attitudes he chooses to adopt to 'the facts'—these facts themselves not being in dispute—is simply not sharing the same conception of morality with the man who believes that 'the facts' cannot always be specified in this morally and metaphysically neutral fashion. I have already suggested that Strawson's conception of morality similarly reflects a particular 'vision of the world.' Thus:

> In short, if moral concepts are regarded as deep moral configurations of the world, rather than as lines drawn round separate factual areas, then there will be no facts 'behind them' for them to be erroneously defined in terms of. There is nothing sinister about this view; freedom here will consist, not in being able to lift the concept off the otherwise unaltered facts and lay it down elsewhere, but in being able to 'deepen' or 'reorganize' the concept or change it for another one. On such a view, it may be noted, moral freedom looks more like a mode of reflection which we may have to achieve, and less like a capacity to vary our choices which we have by definition. I hardly think this a disadvantage.[13]

This notion of a 'vision of life' provides the needed clue to the difficulty of the 'task' of seeing the world as it is. Miss Murdoch in her later work emphasizes the distorting effect upon our vision of the 'fat, relentless ego' and its incessant demand for easy consolation, but she seems to have lost her earlier awareness that there is here an intellectual task to be performed, one which demands spiritual discipline and moral uprightness, but which does not consist in these alone.

Consider, for example, Plato, to whom she constantly refers. Plato too believed that there were elements in the psyche that

[11] *Proc. Ar. Soc.* Supplementary volume, 1956–7, reprinted in *Christian Ethics and Contemporary Philosophy,* ed. I. T. Ramsey, S.C.M. (1966).

[12] *Sartre, Romantic Rationalist,* Cambridge University Press (1953).

[13] *Christian Ethics and Contemporary Philosophy,* pp. 214–15.

tended to deter us from contemplation of the good and distort it, the elements of appetite and uncontrolled self-assertion. But he also believed that there was an exacting intellectual task to be performed by the well ordered soul once it had freed itself from these distorting influences, that of discerning man's nature and man's duty in relation to the entire pattern of the cosmos as ordered by the Good. Hence Plato claimed to be able to show, in principle at least, what the human virtues were, and why they were virtues, and how human society should be organized so as to exemplify them and sustain them. The Christian scheme is, in certain important respects, different from Plato's, but it too represents a more or less articulate 'vision of life', sharing with Platonism the conviction that the ultimate standard is a transcendent one that, here and now at least, we can only dimly apprehend. Miss Murdoch retains the appeal to a transcendent good, but how it illumines and what it illumines she now leaves unsaid. Confronted by the enormous variety of 'pictures of life' which Strawson so vividly evokes, we are given no guidance as to which we should choose or why—only the passionate and somewhat wistful insistence that we may not simply choose as we wish. In consequence Miss Murdoch leaves herself open to the criticism that she once directed upon Sartre. 'It is as if only one certainty remained; that human beings are irreducibly valuable, without any notion why or how they are valuable or how the value can be defended.'[14]

But is this judgement, perhaps, too hasty? For Miss Murdoch gives us a model of the good man's vision—'the unsentimental, detached, unselfish, objective attention' which characterizes the great artist 'a kind of intellectual ability to perceive what is true, which is automatically at the same time a suppression of self.'[15] Indeed she regards it as more than a model; it is itself an *instance* of moral vision: 'appreciation of beauty . . . is a completely adequate entry into (and not just analogy of) the good life, since it *is* the checking of selfishness in the interest of seeing the real.'[16] What can we learn from this comparison?

It is worth reminding ourselves, to begin with, that Walter

[14] *Sartre,* p. 81.
[15] *Sovereignty of Good,* p. 66.
[16] Op. cit., p. 65.

Lippman, as we noticed earlier, makes precisely the same claim for science:

> . . . inside the Laboratory, at the heart of this whole business, the habit of disinterested realism in dealing with the data is the indispensable habit of mind . . . This is an original and tremendous fact in human experience that a whole civilization should be dependent upon pure science, and that this pure science should be dependent upon a race of men who consciously refuse, as Mr Bertrand Russell has said, to regard their 'own desires, tasks and interests as affording a key to the understanding of the world'.[17]

Inspired by this theme Lippman does not hesitate to claim: 'It is no exaggeration to say that pure science is high religion incarnate.'[18] Nor is this claim totally absurd. It is true that the scientist in his professional activity must ignore his personal wishes and submit himself to the arbitrament of the facts, and no amount of rhetoric about 'the myth of the objective consciousness' can controvert this truth.[19] But in this instance it is immediately apparent that scientific disinterestedness is no guarantee of moral rectitude. It is too specialized; it involves too little of the scientist's personality, for the scientist's world is not the only world there is. And should the scientist in fact extend his professional objectivity to his personal and social life it would become inhuman. No one wants to be a perpetual subject for disinterested scientific scrutiny, as Eliza Doolittle discovered.

But would it be any better to be the perpetual object of an equally disinterested aesthetic contemplation? Can such contemplation, any more than that of the scientist, be identified with the love which seeks the good of another and is able to discern it? To be loved is not to be viewed with any sort of detachment, whether scientific or aesthetic.

Iris Murdoch would have been wiser to content herself with drawing an analogy between the artist and the good man. It is true that both art and moral virtue require disinterestedness, but beyond that the analogy has serious limitations. Not all great artists display the 'just and compassionate vision' of which she speaks; or, if she wishes to claim that they do, the

[17] *Preface to Morals,* p. 238., quoted on p. 26. [18] Op. cit., p. 239.

[19] The reference is to Theodore Rosjak, *The Making of a Counter Culture,* chapter VII.

words have to be used in a special sense. Shakespeare and Homer are both indisputably great, so are Rembrandt and the sculptor of the pediment at Olympia; but there is present in Shakespeare and Rembrandt a quality of pity and forgiveness which is missing in the other two. So Helen Gardner can write: 'I find in the ethical temper of Shakespearean tragedy, with its emphasis on pity as the great human virtue, and in the images he so constantly presents of love as a giving not an asking, a distinctively Christian conception of human goodness'.[20] And Kenneth Clark, after noting the unsparing realism of Rembrandt's nude, 'Bathsheba', adds: 'Moreover this Christian acceptance of the unfortunate body has permitted the Christian privilege of a soul.'[21] Both Shakespeare and Homer see without fantasy or self-concern, but what they see is not the same. Compare, for example, the scene in which Lear is reconciled with Cordelia with that in which Achilles receives the suppliant Priam. There are no greater moments in literature, but they belong in different moral worlds.

Moreover, the detachment and the compassion which the great artist manifests as artist is not related in any straightforward way to his moral character as a man and, indeed, to his selfishness or unselfishness as a man. We should like to believe that Tolstoi, in whose novels a 'just and compassionate vision' is more continuously apparent than in any other novelist, displayed in his life the selflessness and detachment of which Iris Murdoch speaks, but it was not so. His ego was too solid and muscular to be described as 'fat', but it was certainly relentless. In her estimate of the artist as man Miss Murdoch is in some danger of being beguiled by the 'consolatory fantasies' she so austerely condemns in the religious. Plato was more realistic in his fears of an irresoluble conflict between morality and art. It is all too apparent that a man may give imaginative expression in his art to a vision of life which is not embodied in his life.

But, in any case, disinterestedness or selflessness is not enough. It does not automatically guarantee an active sympathetic concern with the needs of others. It may be the product of a stoic *apatheia* or a Buddhist annihilation of desire.

[20] *Religion and Literature,* Faber & Faber (1971), p. 79.
[21] *The Nude, A Study in Ideal Form,* Murray (1956), p. 328.

Consider, for example, Sir Arthur Keith's account of the Buddhist attitude to giving:

> The giver must not give for any personal advantage; he must practice what he is to realize in theory, the absence of difference between himself and others . . . But . . . it must be accommodated to the system, and, if this forbids egoism, it equally forbids altruism, and sees no merit in the simply pity of the human heart for distress. Altruism implies existence and is therefore fatal; there is no perfection, compassion, morality, patience, energy, concentration, unless it be permeated by the essential intuition of nothingness; otherwise these virtues are blind and unavailing. The gift, therefore, . . . must be born of compassion, but also of vacuity.[22]

Lack of interest in self may spring from lack of interest in selves.

The conclusion must be that the artist provides a model for morality only if the vision of life to which he gives expression is both profound and true and he actually lives according to it; and this pushes the inquiry back to Iris Murdoch's earlier concern with the choice and validation of forms of life. Otherwise the transcendent good remains empty, notwithstanding her protestations to the contrary.

It is this lack which Stuart Hampshire promises to supply. Hampshire's target is utilitarianism and his chief complaint against it is that it ranges all moral considerations along a single scale of gains and losses and so encourages large scale political computations and a consequent 'coarseness and grossness of moral feeling, a blunting of sensibility, and a suppression of individual discrimination and gentleness.' In this he is in line with other critics of rational humanism in its scientific form. In particular he accuses it of neglecting, indeed, repudiating a certain feature of familiar moralities:

> There are a number of different moral prohibitions . . . which a man acknowledges and which he thinks of as more or less insurmountable, except in abnormal, painful and improbable circumstances. One expects to meet [them] in certain quite distinct and clearly marked areas of action; these are the taking of human life, sexual relations, family duties and obligations and the administration of justice . . . When specific prohibitions in these areas are probed and challenged by reflection, and the rational grounds for them looked for, the questioner will think that he is questioning a particular morality specified by particular prohibitions.

[22] *Buddhist Philosophy in India and Ceylon,* Clarendon Press (1923), p. 250. Keith's interpretation of Buddhism is, doubtless, controversial, but this does not affect the philosophical point.

But if he were to question the validity of any prohibitions in these areas, he would think of himself as challenging the claims or morality itself.[23]

The utilitarian would accept this as a phenomenological description of popular morality but would insist that it be subjected to rational criticism. Some of these prohibitions could, no doubt, be justified on utilitarian grounds. What cannot be thus justified should be discarded, or relegated to a realm of purely personal morality.

Hampshire, it seems, is not content with this solution. While he concedes that proof is unattainable in such matters, he believes that there may nevertheless be 'good reflective reasons' for adopting a particular morality even when it lacks utilitarian support:

. . . in the sense that one is able to say why the conduct is impossible as destroying the ideal of a way of life that one aspires to and respects, as being, for example, utterly unjust or cruel or treacherous or dishonest. To show that these vices are vices, and unconditionally to be avoided, would take us back to the criteria for the assessment of persons as persons, and therefore to the whole way of life that one aspires to as the best way of life.[24]

Thus a moral system falls into two parts, 'a picture of the activities necessary to an ideal way of life which is aspired to, and . . . the unavoidable duties and necessities without which even the elements of human worth, and of a respectworthy way of life are lacking.'[25] In this way Hampshire arrives at a conception of morality closely resembling that to which we were led in the course of examining Strawson's version of liberal humanism. There are certain areas of human life which are universally, or almost universally, subject to moral constraint. The precise formulation of these constraints is determined by ideals which are not arbitrarily chosen but are shaped in accordance with our conception of what is properly human. It follows that Hampshire cannot countenance two of Strawson's central doctrines; the separation of the realms of the moral and the ethical, and the indefinite tolerance extended to incompatible ways of life so long as they do not encroach upon the basic social morality. It is true that 'a reasonable man may envisage a way of life, which excludes various kinds of

[23] *Morality and Pessimism*, reprinted in *Public and Private Morality*, ed. Hampshire, Cambridge University Press (1978), p. 7.

[24] Op. cit., p. 10.

[25] Op. cit., p. 15.

conduct as impossible, without excluding a great variety of morally tolerable ways of life within this minimum framework.'[26] But the minimum framework in question is more extensive than Strawson's basic social morality, because it reflects, as Strawson's does not, 'the ideal of a way of life'.

If the virtues typical of different ways of life cannot be fully combined, and if these ways of life have a social dimension, a very much higher degree of moral consensus is presupposed than the liberal humanist desires. And it seems that they *must* have a social dimension, since they bear upon such matters as respect for life, the administration of justice, sexual behaviour and the regulation of property. In respect of all such matters choices have to be made that are not simply individual choices.

On what basis, then, are such choices to be made? They cannot be, as the romantic humanist would claim, an expression merely of the individual's will; nor does there exist, as the scientific humanist maintains, a science of society which can make them for us. The liberal humanist has no viable alternative to offer. It is of crucial importance, therefore, for the humanist to consider this question and it is not the least of the virtues of Hampshire's essay that he makes at least a preliminary attempt to do this.

He takes as his example the most basic and universal moral prohibition, that on killing. He is not content with a utilitarian theory which reduces the horror of killing to the horror of causing other losses, principally of possible happiness (and this would include any theory which bases it merely upon the preservation of society). Life is not to be valued merely on account of the experiences and satisfactions it makes possible. It is, in a sense, sacred. The problem is, in what sense. The passage in which he deals with this question deserves to be quoted in full:

> Respect for human life, independent of the use made of it, may seem to utilitarians a survival of a sacramental consciousness or at least a survival of a doctrine of the soul's destiny, or the unique relation between God and man. It had been natural to speak of the moral prohibitions against the taking of life as being respect for the sacredness of an individual life; and this phrase has no proper place, it is very reasonably assumed, in the thought of anyone who has rejected belief in supernatural sanctions.

[26] Op. cit., p. 12.

But the situation may be more complicated. The sacredness of life, so called, and the absolute prohibitions against the taking of life, except under strictly defined conditions, may be admitted to be human inventions. Once the human origin of the prohibitions has been recognized, the prohibition against the taking of life, and respect for human life as such, may still be reaffirmed as absolute. They are reaffirmed as complementary to a set of customs, habits and observances, which are understood by reference to their function, and which are sustained, partly because of, partly in spite of, this understanding: I mean sexual customs, family observances, ceremonial treatment of the dead, gentle treatment of those who are diseased and useless, and of the old and senile, customs of war and treatment of prisoners, treatment of convicted criminals, political and legal safeguards for the rights of individuals, and the customary rituals of respect and gentleness in personal dealings. This complex of habits, and the rituals associated with them, are carried over into a secular morality which makes no existential claims that a naturalist would dispute, and which still rejects the utilitarian morality associated with naturalism.[27]

Hampshire here sets out, firmly and sensitively, the lineaments of the European moral tradition at its best, acknowledges its historical involvement with Christianity and vindicates the right of the humanist to reaffirm it without appeal to any supernatural warrant, for, even if its human origin is conceded, respect for human life 'may still be reaffirmed as absolute.'

But what is the force of this 'may'? It appears at first sight to give the prohibition against the taking of life an optional character which it did not have in the tradition to be reaffirmed. There it was a categorical demand; and reasons were given why this value was affirmed as absolute. Is Hampshire in the end reduced to reaffirming the tradition as a Strawsonian 'individual ideal' which others are at liberty to repudiate? It would seem not, for he goes on to insist: 'The question cannot be evaded: what is the rational basis for acting as if human life has a peculiar value, quite beyond the value of any other natural things . . .'[28] This rational basis is not exhausted by the social function which the prohibition performs. It does not, that is to say, belong entirely to Strawson's basic social morality:

The reasons that lead a reflective man to prefer one code of manners, and one legal system, to another must be moral reasons; that is, he must find his reasons in the kind of life that he praises and admires and he aspires to have, and in the kind of person that he wants to become.

[27] Op. cit., p. 17–18.

[28] Op. cit., p. 20.

Reasons for the most general moral choices, which may sometimes be choices among competing moralities, must be found in philosophical reasoning, if they are found at all: that is, in considerations about the relation of men, to the natural, or to the supernatural, order.[29]

What would these reasons be like? Hampshire cannot in the span of a single lecture do more than indicate the considerations that weigh with him. Indeed he mentions only one consideration:

One may on reflection find a particular set of prohibitions and injunctions, and a particular way of life protected by them, acceptable and respectworthy, partly because this specifically conceived way of life, with its accompanying prohibitions, has in history appeared natural, and on the whole still feels natural, both to oneself and to others. If there are no overriding reasons for rejecting this way of life . . . its felt and proven naturalness is one reason among others for accepting it.[30]

We are, however, given little guidance as to what this appeal to 'naturalness' involves. It appears to have no affinities with an earlier form of rational humanism, of which we found vestiges in Kant, according to which moral values are derived from our understanding of what God or Nature intended man to be. Hampshire mentions with approval Spinoza, of whom (in his study of Spinoza) he writes: 'To think of things or persons as fulfilling, or failing to fulfil, a purpose or design is, to imply the existence of a creator distinct from his creation: this is [for Spinoza] a demonstrably meaningless conception.'[31] The appeal to naturalness can take another form, where what is 'natural' is what has come to seem so through the gradual development of a historical tradition. And this interpretation is suggested by Hampshire's reference to 'what in history has appeared natural'. Would Hampshire feel sympathy with Burke's evocation of the English character as the norm of naturalness?

We have real hearts of flesh and blood beating in our bosoms. We fear God; we look up with awe to kings; with affection to Parliaments; with duty to magistrates; with reverence to priests; and with respect to nobility. Why? Because, when such ideas are brought before our minds it is *natural* to be so affected.[32]

I scarcely think so. It is significant, however, that Hampshire

[29] Op. cit., p. 21. [30] Op. cit., p. 21. [31] *Spinoza*, Penguin (1951) p. 111.
[32] *Reflections on the Revolution in France*, University Tutorial Press, p. 89.

feels the need to relate morality to nature, in some sense or other of that notoriously problematic word, and hopes that it may provide some kind of transcendent standard.[33]

It remains to apply what we have learned from these secular critics of prevailing types of humanism to our earlier discussion. We started with the confusion that is everywhere apparent in our moral thinking and reflected in our moral vocabulary, and have traced it to the coexistence of rival moral traditions, each in a kind of dialectical tension with the others and each depending, more or less explicitly, upon a conception of human nature and a corresponding doctrine about man's position in the universe; each morality presupposing an anthropology; each anthropology a metaphysic. The entire argument converges upon Hampshire's conclusion that 'reasons for the most general moral choices, including choices among competing moralities, must be found in philosophical reasoning, if they are to be found at all; *that is in considerations about the relation of men to the natural or to the supernatural order.*'[34] This general pattern is, as Hampshire recognizes, capable of being exemplified by a religious as well as by a secular ethic. Both Hampshire and Iris Murdoch show themselves aware of

[33] Hampshire has since developed his suggestion about nature in an extended essay entitled *Two Theories of Morality* (Thank-offering to Britain Fund Lectures, 1976).

Nature is conceived on the lines of Spinoza as an intelligible order of causes and effects in terms of which the character and significance of human life is to be understood. The enlightened man delights in the discovery and contemplation of the natural order, and is freed from anxious self-concern and the sway of passion to the extent that he appreciates their causes. The way of life to be protected by morality is that of intellectual discovery and inquiry, and it is Hampshire's belief that the prohibitions needed to protect this way of life, and the virtues it sustains and is substained by, will generally coincide with the demands of Western liberal morality.

It is far from obvious why this should be so. Consider Hampshire's earlier, and crucial question: 'What is the rational basis for acting as if human life has a peculiar value quite beyond the value of any other natural things . . . ?' He now writes (expounding and endorsing Spinoza); 'Clearing one's mind of confusions and superstitious fears will always involve getting rid of the idea of oneself as an original cause and as a sovereign will and as an island in nature.' But this merging of man in nature with its explicit rejection of the Kantian emphasis on autonomy and its almost Buddhist denial of the self would seem to dispose, not only of specifically Christian, but also of broadly humanist reasons for regarding human life as of peculiar value. If I myself am not an original cause or an 'island in nature', no more is any other man. Where selves as such have so little significance, there is no more warrant for altruism than there is for egoism.

[34] My italics.

the existence of a religious alternative, and both take it for granted, without reason given, that such an alternative is to be rejected. Yet it can scarcely escape notice that their own criticisms of prevailing secular moralities are such as a specifically religious thinker might well advance. And I think it is not unfair to say that, in the case of both of them there is a certain awkwardness in their avoidance of religious themes. The Good, as Iris Murdoch conceives it, really does look like a severely attenuated God (a sort of Cheshire Cat's smile); and, Hampshire has palpable difficulty in divesting his language about the sanctity of human life of its Christian associations. Moreover it is apparent that the emptiness of Iris Murdoch's idea of the Good is attributable to the absence of the sort of metaphysical framework that might have given it substance and the need for which she argued so eloquently in her earlier work. And even if Hampshire's suggestions for supplying that need get little beyond tentative exploratory gestures, they reinforce our sense of that need.

The two thinkers I have been considering are representative of many other thoughtful people in their possession of what one may call a traditional conscience. It tells them that certain sorts of conduct are wrong in all, or almost all, circumstances; that it is of supreme importance that they as individuals should become and remain certain sorts of people and that the society to which they belong should exemplify certain standards; and that these moral demands upon them are not the expression simply of choices made by them or by their society, but are in some important sense objective and categorical. And they are faced with the question what view of man and what conception of man's place in the universe can make sense of such a conscience; and whether, if no acceptable rationale for it is on offer, they should regard it as obsolete and give it up.

6

The Dilemma of the Traditional Conscience

I have noted the dissatisfaction of certain sensitive minds with prevailing patterns of secular morality. What they look for in them, and do not find, is a standard that transcends the *de facto* preferences of individuals and societies, by which these may be judged; the recognition of ideals or principles to which a man may be seriously and continuously committed, and upon which greater emphasis is laid than would be justifiable on utilitarian grounds alone. They have, that is to say, a conception of moral character, which is out of phase with the moral theories that are available to them.

For the utilitarian a good man can only be one who acts rightly in every situation, that is to say who makes a correct calculation as to what, in that situation, is likely to produce the best results. But a man whose sole motive is this generalized benevolence cannot develop any fundamental consistency of character, for any virtues he might achieve, any loyalties he might acknowledge, any ideals he might subscribe to, would inevitably tend to distract him from his single-minded devotion to utility. For just the same reason this attitude is a solvent of institutional ties and personal relationships. It atomizes the individual and the institutions to which he belongs and, in the guise of securing his happiness or furthering his purposes, drastically curtails the range and depth of the happiness that is open to him and the purposes that he is able to contemplate. For we normally think of our happiness as consisting in such things as being, for example, happily married or happy in our work, and our purposes include such things as marrying a particular person or achieving a particular job. And both of these presuppose a whole web of obligations and loyalties. Indeed so does 'the situation' in which at any time we have to act. Try describing a difficult situation in which you have need of advice and you will find yourself mentioning such things as your special relationship to A, your promise to B, the legitimate interests of C. The trouble with 'situation ethics' is precisely that it does not do justice to situations.

The standard utilitarian response to this line of argument is to claim that the enlightened utilitarian will, of course, recognize that certain dispositions, certain special relationships, certain institutional frameworks, with their associated obligations, will tend on balance to promote the general happiness and are to be encouraged for this reason. The trouble is, however, that they will not have this effect unless the individual takes them seriously and allows his personality to be profoundly and permanently modified by them, and it is just this that is incompatible with his at the same time subjecting them to a steady utilitarian monitoring. As Bernard Williams puts it, in a persuasive development of this theme, the effect of the utilitarian approach is 'to alienate him in a real sense from his actions and the source of his action in his own convictions'. This is so because the man himself 'is identified with his actions as flowing from projects and attitudes which in some cases he takes seriously at the deepest level'.[1] The same sort of difficulty arises with spontaneity. On the face of it the utilitarian is constantly on duty, ready at any and every moment to shift the total balance of happiness by doing or refraining from doing some relevant action—and every action or omission may be relevant. Spontaneity seems ruled out. Of course the utilitarian will allow, indeed recommend, a certain measure of spontaneity as likely to have better results than continuous calculation. Yet, once again, the trouble is that such licensed and carefully rationed spontaneity will not meet our need; it is uncomfortably like the relaxed manner of the television personality, too 'professional' to be wholly convincing. Thus both the needs to which he ministers and the motives from which he acts are conceived by the utilitarian in too jejune a fashion to match the variety and the solidity of human life.

It is a sense of this impoverishment that inspires the romantic revolt against rational humanism, but in a different way it too dissolves the individual in whom it seeks to vest so much significance. If each man is to choose his values for himself in sovereign independence, he is left with no reason for the

[1] *Utilitarianism For and Against*, p. 116.

choices he makes and no need to develop a consistent policy from one moment to another. The typical romantic emphasis upon the autonomy of the will and the authenticity of the emotions militates against the imposition of any lasting pattern, even a self-imposed one. Character necessarily involves restraining immediate impulses for the sake of some long term good; and it is hard to see how character can be developed without the individual passing through a stage at which his feelings and his intentions do not yet match his principles. And this necessary process of development can scarcely occur without a background of shared and settled values with its appropriate institutional setting. But these are things that the romantic humanist sees as essentially hostile to the realization of the individual personality, seducing him towards heteronomy and *mauvaise foi*. In this the liberal humanist in the end concurs. The limited concession that he is prepared to make towards the requirements of social life—the basic minimum morality—is carefully circumscribed so as to prevent its influencing the individual at any deep level. For to allow it to do so would be to encroach upon the domain of ideals, which is the preserve of purely personal choice.

For illustration of the effect of this we need only consider, once again, the predicament of universities, whose traditional ethic is under continuous pressure both from government and from students. The government pressures are utilitarian, insisting on cost-effectiveness, measuring performance by the achievement of results statistically assessed, looking for more efficient means of achieving these results. The average university teacher, when confronted with this approach, is merely bewildered. His entire idea of himself as a teacher in a community of scholars, to which he has devoted his life, involves too many imponderables that cannot be caught by the official statistics or articulated in the official language. The qualities to which his obituary will pay tribute are almost wholly irrelevant to this official conception of his role. The students—or, at any rate, those who represent them—are, as a rule, romantics. The traditional institutions of the university, its conventions and its etiquette, which the don sees as embodying and helping to preserve its characteristic ethos, they regard as unacceptable constraints upon their own creative freedom, and, by challenging in its name every feature of university life, which cannot be given the plainest sort of utilitarian justification, they ally themselves, in effect, although not in intention, with the university's most philistine opponents.

It is not surprising, therefore, that the word 'character' itself has acquired a somewhat old-fashioned air. It presupposes that a man has, implicitly or explicitly, a conception of what he should be and of what others may rightly expect him to be; that he has principles which he will not readily betray, that he has loyalties and affections of an enduring kind; that he is subject to temptations which he is prepared to resist; that he accepts responsiblity for his actions and expects other people to accept responsibility for theirs. Such a man fits uneasily into the world of the utilitarian, because he has too much psychic property for the kind of ethical mobility that world requires. And he is equally unsuited to the world of the liberal or romantic humanist for he cannot regard all this merely as a matter of personal preference.

The situation is recognized–and illuminated–in John Bayley's book, *The Characters of Love*. Bayley takes as his subject the decline of character in modern literature, particularly the novel. He distinguishes between 'nature' and 'the human condition'. 'The subject matter may even be the same, but those who write about Nature take it for granted, while those who write about the Human Condition take an attitude towards it'.[2] One might say that writing about 'the human condition' is essentially a romantic activity whereas 'nature', as Bayley understands it in the context of literature, represents an agreed moral order, which has now disintegrated. 'The critic's distrust of judging in terms of "character" today', Bayley writes, 'arises from the total absence of agreement about what people are really like and how they can be portrayed.'[3] The romantic 'could only work through the detached and "interesting" personality, since the moral order which made such a character nugatory, except in so far as he conformed or failed to conform to it, had lost all general authority . . . Such a full-blooded pursuit of personality . . . separates the relished individual from the social and moral background

[2] *The Characters of Love*, p. 269.
[3] Op. cit., p. 281.

of the old order of nature.'[4] We can see what Bayley has in mind if we take Jane Austen's judgement on Elizabeth Bridges in a letter to her sister, Cassandra: 'We need not enter into a Panegyric on the Departed – but it is sweet to think of her great worth – of her solid principles, her true devotion, her excellence in every relation of life,'[5] and compare it with some remarks of Philip Toynbee's in a review of a biography of P. G. Wodehouse:

> . . . Wodehouse may not have had any depths to be explored. This is a heresy, of course, for we are all inclined to suspect that even the blandest of exteriors must conceal some sort of pandemonium within: indeed we believe that the blander the mask the more violent the turbulence which it is intended to conceal. We forget that there are men and women who really are what they appear to be; who have no lurid secrets to hide either from us or from themselves; who exist quite happily on the surface of things.[6]

It is this last phrase that is so revealing. Toynbee seems to take it entirely for granted that only a shallow personality can be what it appears to be, and that depths must be turbulent. What, in that case, we may well ask, of Jane Austen herself?

The contrast is familiar to us in television. One has only to compare the serial versions of Trollope, or Thackeray or Tolstoi with the typical 'Play for Today' to notice the massive solidity of the nineteenth-century character in contrast with the shapelessness of those innumerable variations upon John Osborne's Jimmy Porter. One could say about the modern playwright what Bayley says about the novelist: 'Our communion with the usual novelist is essentially a communion of earnestness and of badness, of responding to these in him and in ourselves. But Nature always has the proportions of goodness.'[7]

Bayley uses the word 'nature' in a somewhat idiosyncratic way to stand for an accepted order of society, and one reason for the present moral confusion is no doubt the decay of such an order. Indeed Alasdair MacIntyre traces the liberal emphasis on the secondary virtues of co-operativeness, fair play, and tolerance to the existence of a number of competing class

[4] Op. cit., p. 282.

[5] *Jane Austen's Letters,* ed. R. W. Chapman, Oxford University Press (1934), p. 220.

[6] *Observer,* 24 Aug. 1975.

[7] Op. cit., p. 286.

moralities which stand in the way of any agreement in our society about substantial aims.

> In this soil is rooted the liberal belief that facts are neutral because facts can be impersonally and objectively established, but values are personal, values are private, values can be chosen. This liberal attitude is one which all the different, conflicting groups have needed to invoke in order to protect themselves against the overriding claims of the others, but which at the same time undermines any assertion that they might otherwise feel able to make about the overriding character of their own values.[8]

MacIntyre discovers the origin of this state of affairs in purely social developments which make the idea of a moral authority no longer a viable one, but his own analysis suggests that the situation is more complicated than that. The breakdown of a common morality helped to bring about a process of social disintegration, by which it was in turn accelerated. But this decline in moral authority was associated with certain changes in belief.

It has often been remarked that the Victorians, whether believers, atheists, or agnostics, possessed a massive confidence in the importance and validity of conscience; and that this, together with their emphasis on character, derived from a Christian tradition. What is less often noticed—or seen as significant—is that this tradition had incorporated certain pagan themes. Chief among these was the conception of a common human nature unified by reason. Reason, thus understood, enables a man to grasp intellectually what is the good for man, and why it is good, in relation to his place in the universe, so that he can direct his will aright and school his emotions to be appropriate to their objects.

The Stoic version of this theme, as it was revived in the eighteenth century, steadily removed the supernatural from its controlling position and tended almost to identify the order of nature itself with the divine reason. Yet the affect upon ethics was comparatively slight, since, despite the rejection of orthodoxy, it was still possible to think of human nature as having its part to play in a natural order that was purposive. The enormous authority of the idea of nature throughout this period is associated with its independence of mere human vagary and custom. Thus, for many eighteenth-

[8] *Secularization and Moral Change*, p. 45.

century thinkers, to say, with Hampshire, that 'reasons for the most general moral choices . . . must be found in philosophical reasoning, if they are found at all: that is, in considerations about the relation of men, to the natural or to the supernatural, order', would scarcely have been to pose distinct alternatives. Human nature was securely part of the natural order, which whether or not it was created by God, had its own immanent rationality. Thus when Jefferson, in the opening sentences of the *Declaration of Independence,* refers to 'the laws of Nature and of Nature's God', he comes very close to identifying the two.

Hence it was possible to divest oneself of specifically Christian beliefs, or even of any very explicit theism, without appearing to disturb the broad pattern of morality, based upon a human nature thought of as firmly embedded in the natural order. It was entirely consistent with this that the task of exploring and extending man's knowledge of his own nature should devolve increasingly upon science. The orthodox could and did regard this as a way of uncovering God's purposes, while the enlightened relied upon it as an alternative to revealed religion. In either case what was being discovered was thought of as entirely objective and independent of human choices, and the relationship between moral character and moral discernment remained essentially unchanged.

Putting it very simply, the pagan philosophy to which the enlightened could appeal against Christianity, had enough in common with Christianity, to enable a substantially Christian ethic, based on a substantially Christian conception of human nature, to survive the repudiation of much, or even all, explicitly Christian doctrine. And this was assisted by the ambiguity of the term 'nature', which retained its reassuring suggestions of normativeness, and transcendence of merely human fashions, yet could range from the teleological to the purely descriptive, from the scientific to the mystical.

What seems to have brought about our own very different situation is that, at varying rates and in diverse ways, in England and on the continent of Europe, this confidence in a common human nature began to break down, and with it the traditional idea of moral character. To document this process would require an excursus into cultury history, for which I have neither space nor competence. Yet consideration of it cannot be entirely omitted. Although my concern is philosophical, one cannot discuss philosophical issues in a cultural vacuum. Concepts have a history and cannot be adequately understood apart from it. As it happens the theme is central to John Weightman's fascinating study, *The Concept of the Avant-Garde.*[9] Weightman sees the Enlightenment as the chief formative episode in the modern world, and claims that by the end of the eighteenth century in France the modern evolutionary and secular view of the world had pervaded the consciousness of the intellectual élite. For the French *philosophes*

> if history was such a record of crime and injustice, this was because it had not been conducted in accordance with the true nature of man. Once man had been defined as a natural phenomenon like other natural phenomena, without all the mystical accretions of the past, society would right itself, and the generations of the future would find themselves in a social context that would allow the full and harmonious expression of their inherent possibilities.[10]

The phenomenon of the avant-garde, in Weightman's view, owes its existence to the fact that the Enlightenment hope of achieving a definition of human nature has come to seem more and more illusory:

> Consequently it would take a very confident man today to echo the line from Terence which was a slogan of 19th century humanism: *Homo sum, humani nihil a me alienum puto.* In other words, as some modern thinkers – particularly French ones – like to put it, the death of God is now being followed by the death of Man. . . . The sheer fact of living in time becomes then an existential anguish, because history is no more than a succession of moments, all in a way equally valid or invalid, and human nature ceases to be a unifying concept and is no more than the name we give to the successive appearances of man.[11]

And so we have the reaction that I have been calling 'romantic humanism' which has, among its varied manifestations, as Weightman observes, a widespread disgust with the idea of science, the search for the sensation of mystic depth, an apparently meaningful, though incomprehensible, relationship to the transcendent.[12] The predicament to which this is the response is precisely that expressed by Iris Murdoch: 'Human life has external point or *telos* . . . There are properly many

[9] Alcove Press (1973).
[10] Op. cit., p. 26.
[11] Op. cit., p. 30.
[12] Op. cit., p. 31.

patterns or purposes within life, but there is no general and as it were generally guaranteed pattern or purpose of the kind for which philosophers and theologians used to search. We are what we seem to be, transient, mortal creatures, subject to necessity and chance.'[13] In this situation Iris Murdoch makes her own heroic appeal to the idea of a transcendent good, using language strongly reminiscent of Plato, but her denial of any 'external point or *telos*' to human life involves as complete a repudiation of Plato and the entire pagan tradition to which the *philosophes* appealed as it does of Christianity itself.

In England the radically secular spirit took hold much more gradually than on the continent so that the more extreme reaction was long delayed. God, so to speak, was much longer dying. But one can see the same predicament as it affected one of the least insular Englishmen of his age, Matthew Arnold. And here I rely chiefly on Lionel Trilling's early study of him. Trilling comments, in language very similar to Iris Murdoch's: 'Arnold, looking into the chasm which had once been filled by the poetry of a belief in the divine origin of man and the world, feels, no less than the romantics, the difficulty of a life in which man has no point beyond himself to which he may refer his action, thought and aspiration.'[14] Like all the great Victorians, Arnold had no doubt as to what was right and wrong, nor as to the categorical demand of conscience. Morality is summed up in a very traditional way as 'Kindness and purity, charity and chastity'. His problem was to find a satisfactory rationale for his convictions and a framework that could give meaning and purpose to his life. His solution was to reinterpret Christianity in a way that strikingly anticipates some of our contemporary theologians. Thus in *St. Paul and Protestantism* he asserts: 'All that is conceptual in Paul, all that is theoretical, all that touches the realm of science, is unscientific, secondary and to be passed over. All that is emotional, all that is experiential, is primary and in conformity with science.'[15] Yet this appeal to emotion and experience alone is not enough to provide a basis for morality. In order

[13] *The Sovereignty of Good*, p. 79, quoted in chapter 5, p. 66 above.
[14] Lionel Trilling, *Matthew Arnold*, George Allen & Unwin (1955), p. 96.
[15] *St. Paul and Protestantism*, quoted in Trilling, op. cit., p. 350.

to achieve that it is necessary to characterize further what it is that is experienced, how it is the appropriate object of our religious emotions, and in what way it guarantees righteousness. So Arnold speaks of the God of the Jews as 'the power not ourselves that makes for righteousness'[16] and tells us that this power is the creative source of morality itself. He speculates about the first man to feel the stirrings of conscience, and asks:

> Who first, amid the loose solicitations of [sexual] sense, obeyed (for create he did not) the mighty *not ourselves* which makes for moral order, the stream of tendency which was here carrying him, and our embryo race along with him, towards the fulfilment of the true law of their being, became aware of it and obeyed it?[17]

The 'not ourselves that makes for righteousness' is not, however, identified by Arnold with the God of traditional theism, which he explicitly rejects. Indeed it is scarcely more than a minimum specification for what might fill the gap left in Arnold's conception of morality by this very rejection. When he endeavours to articulate it further, he slides into incoherence:

> No one will say that it is admittedly certain and verifiable, that there is a personal just cause, the moral and intelligent governor of the universe, whom we may call *God* if we will. But that all things seem to us to have what we call a law of their being, and to tend to fulfil it, is certain and admitted; though whether we will call this *God* or not is a matter of choice. Suppose, however, we called it *God*, we then give the name of *God* to a certain and admitted reality.[18]

Arnold is able to give this argument such semblance of plausibility as it possesses only through an equivocation upon the expression 'law of their being'. If this refers to an immanent 'point or *telos*', which gives human life a purpose, it has some relevance to morality, and could even be identified with God as conceived in a vestigial Stoicism. But then its existence is far from being 'certain and admitted'. If, on the other hand, Arnold is referring to scientific laws governing human nature, they do not, even if they are 'certain and admitted', provide any sufficient basis for ethics.

What is of interest in Arnold for our discussion is not his muddled attempts to solve the problem, but his intense awareness of the problem itself, which shows itself even more

[16] *Literature and Dogma*, quoted in Trilling, p. 356.
[17] *God and the Bible*, quoted in Trilling, p. 355.
[18] *Literature and Dogma*, quoted in Trilling, p. 355.

pervasively in his poetry than in his prose, as in the well-known lines from *Dover Beach*:

> Ah, love, let us be true
> To one another: for the world, which seems
> To lie before us like a land of dreams,
> So various, so beautiful, so new,
> Hath really neither joy, nor love, nor light,
> Nor certitude, nor peace, nor help for pain;
> And we are here as on a darkling plain
> Swept with confused alarms of struggle and flight,
> Where ignorant armies clash by night.

And all the time he hears 'the melancholy, long, withdrawing roar' of the sea of faith. There is an enormous sense of loss. It would not be difficult to document this sense of loss in other thinkers both English and European, the chief difference being that, among the Europeans, its expression was generally more violent. Weightman, for example, writes of Paul Valéry that 'he was perpetually trying to define the essence of life, and since, by definition, he couldn't relate it to any transcendent absolute, his final philosophy is a sort of nihilism.'[19] And even Nietzsche exclaims:

> How greatly we should like to exchange the false assertions of the priests, that there is a God who desires good from us, a guardian and witness of every action, everv moment, every thought, who loves us and seeks our welfare in all misfortune—how greatly we would like to exchange these ideas for truths which would be just as healing, pacifying and beneficial as these errors. But there are no such truths.[20]

Thus we can discern a steady decline since the Enlightenment of the once universal confidence in a common human nature, a process by which the 'death of God' has been succeeded by the 'death of Man'. Whatever may have been 'the acids of modernity' (to use Walter Lippman's phrase) which have brought this about, they have eroded the older forms of rational humanism no less effectively, indeed, perhaps, even more effectively, than they have weakened orthodox Christianity. For the ancient pagan doctrines of man, to which the *philosophes* appealed in their critical assault upon Christianity, were based upon the belief that human reason was a spark of that universal Reason that was immanent in the whole of

[19] Weightman, op. cit., p. 125.

[20] *Human, All-too-Human,* Part one, tr. Helen Zimmern, Russell and Russell (1967), p. 112.

Nature. So morality was based on a purpose written in the nature of things—written so clearly that there was no need of divine assistance to decipher it, and only superstition could obscure it.

Once this belief was undermined by Darwin and those evolutionary theorists who anticipated him, it was still open to Christians to think of man as made in the image of God and as having an immortal destiny in the purposes of God, for these beliefs had never rested upon observation of the natural world alone; but the humanists had no such recourse. They had, therefore, either to look for some new way of justifying their old moral intuitions, or to modify their moral outlook to suit their revised understanding of the human predicament. The continental thinkers, whom Weightman studies, chose the latter course and frankly embraced a romantic doctrine of the individual as the creator of his own values. Matthew Arnold (and to a large extent John Stuart Mill) remained loyal to the old intuitions. Mill found it notoriously difficult to reconcile these with his official utilitarianism, and Arnold preserved a vestigial deity ('a power not ourselves making for righteousness') to act as a sort of ether in which his entirely traditional values could subsist in independence of his own choices. It is hard to resist the conclusion reached by A. O. G. Cockshut in his study of the Victorian agnostics,

> They were not trying to discover how they ought to behave, for their conscience formed by generations of Christianity told them that clearly enough. They were trying to establish *why*, now the religious motive was removed, they ought to behave as their conscience told them.[21]

That this process has occurred as a part of cultural history can scarcely be denied. To that extent the death of God has been followed by the death of Man. But, we are bound to ask, need it be? It may be true that our civilization has been profoundly influenced by the belief that human life has a meaning beyond itself, and that to live rightly is to align oneself with the true direction of human nature as seen in the purposes of God; and that to be deprived of this belief is a severe and, in some individuals, disabling shock. But men can suffer from illusions, even very powerful and long-lasting illusions, and it may be very painful to be forced to recognise them as

[21] *The Unbelievers,* Collins (1964), p. 157.

illusions and to have to face life without them. The point has been made succinctly by Freud: 'A man who has for decades taken a sleeping draught is naturally unable to sleep if he is deprived of it.'

So should we not say that western man has for centuries taken a very potent sleeping draught, inducing dreams of great splendour which were able to impart a feeling of significance to his waking life? If so, must he not school himself to do without? Freud goes on:

> True, man will then find himself in a difficult situation. He will have to confess his utter helplessness and his insignificant part in the working of the universe; he will have to confess that he is no longer the centre of creation, no longer the object of the tender care of a benevolent providence. He will be in the same position as the child who has left the home where he was so warm and comfortable. But, after all, is it not the destiny of childishness to be overcome? Man cannot remain a child forever; he must venture at last into the hostile world.[22]

Here Freud speaks in the authentic tones of rational humanism. And, of course, he may be right. If it is true that the 'death of God' has, among the intelligentsia, led to the 'death of Man' and that this has profoundly affected their conception of morality, it does not necessarily follow that this historical phenomenon represents a rational development. The intelligentsia may simply have been misled. Could it not be, in fact, a massive illustration of the danger that secular thinkers have always suspected from the association of ethics with religion, viz. that the morality tends to be abandoned along with the religion although it is not in any way logically dependent upon it? Can we not learn in the end to sleep better without the sleeping draught, to have a firmer grasp of morality without God?

In the light of our discussion the following answer suggests itself. The most characteristic contemporary forms of secular humanism resemble each other in their failure to provide a rationale for morality as traditionally conceived. In particular they have no place for the conscientious man, the man of character, the man who says 'Ich Kann nicht anders'; or, rather, to the extent that they *can* find a place for him, it is on

[22] *Future of an Illusion*, translated by W. D. Robson-Scott, The International Psycho-Analytical Library (1928), pp. 85-6.

terms that he is bound to reject, such as that it is socially useful for him to become this sort of man, or that he is free, if he so chooses, to become this sort of man, although he need not. They do not, either, give the claims of other men the weight that the traditional moralist feels they ought to have; and this is in part because men are not thought of as possessing the depth and consistency of character that is needed to give their claims this weight. For if men are primarily bearers of experiences or authors of choices, and the experiences of different individuals are interchangeable and their choices arbitrary, it is hard to see why people matter as much as he feels intuitively they do. The 'death of Man' is the death of man as a moral being, faced by the choice of good and evil and held responsible for his choice. And what brought about his death was the growing conviction that, as Iris Murdoch, puts it 'life has no external point or *telos,* a conviction which separates modern man from Christian and pagan alike. It is for this reason that, as C. S. Lewis reminded us, 'A post-Christian man is not a pagan; you might as well think that a married woman recovers her virginity by divorce. The post-Christian is cut off from the Christian past and therefore doubly from the pagan past'[23] If this argument holds good, the intelligentsia were not entirely misled. The man of traditional conscience does indeed face a dilemma. He must be prepared to choose between modifying his conscience and questioning his secular assumptions.

[23] *De Descriptione Temporum* (Inaugural Lecture at Cambridge), C.U.P. (1955), p. 15.

7

Transition to a Religious Ethic; Morality and World-views

At this point an objector might well intervene. 'Your examples to illustrate the decline or character', he might say, 'are drawn very largely from imaginative literature and literary criticism. But the fact that a certain conception of character no longer stimulates the creative artist, is, so to speak, aesthetically played out, does not imply that it no longer has validity in real life. Moreover, even if it is true that certain ways of looking at morality have in our history been so involved with Christianity that many now repudiate them on that account, and those who wish to maintain them find it hard to avoid religious overtones, it does not follow that they depend logically upon Christian belief. Nor, even if they do follow logically from Christian premisses, does this mean that there are not other, non-Christian, premisses from which they equally follow. You have not taken sufficient account of Freud's comment about the effect of awakening from a long dream.'

This objection must, in principle, be accepted. All that the argument so far has done is to render plausible a suggestion. And, so far as the argument goes, there may yet be a form or forms of secular humanism which save the intuitions of the critics as well as, or better than, any form of Christianity can do. It is notoriously hard to prove a negative; and I cannot claim to have enumerated all possible forms of secular humanism. Indeed, it might be argued that no matter what the content of Christian ethics, the entirely secular thinker can always adopt it as his own, without committing himelf on any point of doctrine or of metaphysics. I have spoken of 'intuitions'. Why can he not simply trust his intuitions as such? If he is prepared to be an intuitionist in ethics he need not be troubled by problems of justification. Equally, if he rejects intuitionism in favour of a form of subjectivism, there is nothing to prevent him adopting, as a matter of fundamental ethical choice, just what principles he wishes (so long as he is consistent). In this way too he can take over as much or as little of traditional Christian ethics as he chooses.

The objection can be strengthened still further. Not only are these two alternatives open to the philosopher with a traditional conscience; it can be argued that they are his only possible options. For, if he his not an intuitionist in ethics or a subjectivist, he must be guilty of the so-called naturalistic fallacy. He must, that is, be committed to the view that moral questions can be reduced to questions of fact—either empirical fact or metaphysical fact; and this view has been agreed to be unacceptable, at least since the time of David Hume. In order to reach moral conclusions we must always have moral premisses and in our attempt to justify these we are driven back to certain ultimate moral premisses, which are themselves incapable of justification. It remains then only to ask how we get these ultimate principles, and there are only two answers possible: either we just 'see' that they are true, i.e. we 'intuit' their truth, or we adopt them by our own free choice, realizing that the responsibility for them is entirely our own.

Thus, on the logic of the matter the intuitionist and the subjectivist are agreed. Moral reasoning takes the form of deduction from first principles, which cannot themselves be justified. It is about the epistemology of morals that they differ, about how we know—indeed whether, strictly speaking, we *do* know—what is right or wrong.

Of the two theories intuitionism has the merit of satisfying one deep-seated demand on the part of the man of sensitive conscience, viz. that the claims of conscience should be thought of as binding upon him, whether he likes it or not. When all has been said that *can* be said to mitigate the apparent arbitrariness of subjectivism,[1] it remains the case that, as Williams puts it, 'moral thinking *feels* as though it mirrored something, as though it were constrained to follow, rather than be freely creative'.[2] Nevertheless—notoriously—intuitionism suffers from a number of defects, of which two are particularly serious.

The first is that it leaves unexplained how the various

[1] See Bernard Williams on 'defusing subjectivism', in *Morality*, Penguin (1972), pp. 40 ff.

[2] Op. cit., p. 50.

elements in our morality are related to one another or to the rest of life. There just are, it appears, certain duties which we see to be incumbent upon us, and there is no way, even in principle, in which we can come to understand why we have these duties and not others, and how these duties are connected, (except, perhaps, by reference to certain ends, whose goodness is similarly intuited). Nor is it clear how we can criticize what we thus intuit, or modify our consciences in the light of fresh discoveries. In fact the systematic relationship which we have noticed between moral concepts and world-views becomes a curious and inexplicable sociological phenomenon. So does the connection, so fascinatingly explored by anthropologists, between the social structure and the ethics of primitive societies. It is not the intuitionist's insistence on the objectivity of morality that is called in question by these considerations, but the discontinuity he introduces between morality and the other aspects of human life.

The second is that it does nothing to illuminate the relationship between moral discernment and action. It is hard to see how our recognizing that an action is right or wrong should provide us with a reason or a motive for doing it, or refraining from doing it, unless we can see some connection between the rightness and wrongness of the action and a whole way of life that has meaning for us and engages our interest and concern. We need something like the 'good reflective reasons' for adopting a particular morality of which Hampshire writes.

If these familiar criticisms of intuitionism are valid, as I think they are, the moralist cannot rely simply on his intuitions as entirely self-authenticating; he must provide some rationale of them, or at least allow the need for one. This is not to say, as some utilitarians would, that we can ignore altogether the immediate intuitive judgements which we form when we reflect upon particular situations of difficulty. We are often, most of us, very much better at discerning what considerations are morally relevant in such cases than we are at articulating or justifying the principles upon which we then rely. I should myself, as a general rule, prefer to trust the judgement of an experienced doctor in a matter of medical ethics than that of most moral philosophers. But, if we are prepared to rely upon our own intuitions and those of other people, we must recognize the need to justify the weight we give them against utilitarians like Smart who see no reason why they should be trusted. It is not enough to maintain, as Hampshire does, that utilitarianism violates certain deeply held moral convictions. To this the utilitarian can reply that, given the transparent reasonableness of the utilitarian principle, we are simply being obscurantist in resisting its application in the disputed cases.[3] We need some ground for the importance we attach to intuitions. Aristotle, who was prepared to regard the good man as the 'rule and canon of virtue', had such a ground. For it is, in his view, characteristic of a good man, that is to say a good specimen of a man, that he is reflectively aware, as a good horse, for instance, could not be, of what his goodness requires of him. And even the ordinary man, though not given to philosophical reflection, is as a rational being very much more likely than not to be right about fundamental questions of ethics. So it is wise to take seriously received opinions, and Aristotle does test his general theories of ethics by reference to what is commonly accepted. By contrast the Oxford intuitionists, like Ross, Caritt, and Prichard, provided no adequate reason for taking the deliverances of 'the common moral consciousness' as seriously as they did. Thus, if our sensitive moral critic is to retain his faith in an objective moral demand, and if he is to continue to trust his moral intuitions (including his intuition that morality is objective), he needs a more comprehensive theory of ethics than intuitionism provides, one that makes it intelligible that morality should be responsive to what we know or believe about man and the world, and which can explain how morality is related to action and choice. The appeal to intuition, though legitimate as far as it goes, cannot relieve us of the task of defending whatever conception we choose to have of the nature, scope and content of morality. The ethical discussion itself demands to be extended, if not to religion, at least to the metaphysics of ethics.

No doubt one of the reasons for the reluctance of contemporary thinkers, whose moral intuitions are of a profoundly traditional kind, to countenance any serious consideration of religion, is a residual suspicion of metaphysics. Yet, as we have

[3] Cf. J. J. C. Smart, *Utilitarianism For and Against,* p. 56.

seen, even Strawson, with all his careful avoidance of dogmatism, exhibits a recognizable 'vision of life'. On examining his version of liberal humanism we found that it rested upon what he himself would call 'a profound general statement about man and the universe'. According to it, man is a being who, once certain basic needs are satisfied, is free to create for himself ideals of excellence which make each man what he is. There are no objective criteria by which these may be judged, nor is any consistency over time demanded. Men may, and often do, devise religious and metaphysical schemes in terms of which to justify their ideals, but these too, are not capable of being strictly true or false. In order to satisfy his inescapable needs and free himself to realize his ideals, whatever they are, a man requires a society, and this in turn demands a basic minimum morality. Strawson implies, I think, that men are under an obligation to observe the rules of this basic morality, and that toleration of other people's ideals (so long as they do not endeavour to engross the common morality) is, if not actually obligatory, at least clearly indicated by his total scheme. The man who is at home in the liberal society will be the man who identifies himself in imagination with the ideals of others, even if he does not share them. Thus it is not hard to see that Strawson's moral judgements fit his ethical theory, and that his ethical theory is governed by his conception of what it is to be a man. The whole assumes a broadly empiricist theory about the limits of what can be said to be true or false; and, although this theory dictates that Strawson's 'vision of life' cannot be true but only 'profoundly true', it constitutes a metaphysic, albeit a somewhat exiguous one.

Our entire discussion suggests that this pattern is not peculiar to Strawson, but will be discernible in any coherent view of ethics. In discussing different moral viewpoints at all thoroughly we shall be led to examine the 'visions of life' which they reflect and the philosophical assumptions which they presuppose; and until this is done, it will not be possible to make a rational choice between them. (Whether such a rational choice is possible at all, will be itself one of the questions at issue.)

It cannot, therefore, be made a reasonable ground of complaint against a religious ethic that it involves metaphysical assumptions, for this is true of any system of ethics. It is a mistake to identify secular morality with 'morality' *tout court,* taken as entirely straightforward and unproblematic, while associating religious morality with a host of controversial assumptions of a metaphysical kind. To the extent that a non-controversial morality can be discerned—the morality of the platitudes—it falls short of the practical requirements of any civilized society, indeed of any society at all; nor does it satisfy many of our more discriminating moral intuitions, unless it is interpreted in ways that render it no longer uncontroversial. Moreover large questions remain unanswered about the extent to which its claims are binding upon us, and the reasons why we should regard ourselves as bound by them.

If morality has a metaphysical dimension in the way I have described, it is evident that awkward problems arise about the autonomy of ethics. To what extent, in choosing between world-views, should we be influenced by their ethical implications? If, on other than ethical grounds, we are inclined to accept a particular account of the nature of man and his place in the universe, how far should we be deterred from embracing it by the fact that it yields moral conclusions which we find objectionable. If we are deterred, how can this response of ours be justified?

The task before us is, therefore, one of rather alarming complexity. The confusion and controversy about morality (which I tried to document in my opening chapter) infects every level of thinking about morality, and very little can be assumed in advance to be agreed by the participants in the debate. It is like playing croquet with flamingoes.

Perhaps it may help if we make use of a very simple model which is exemplified in a number of introductions to moral philosophy. There are three storeys on which morality may be discussed. On the ground floor are ordinary people—'plain men'—making comparatively unreflective moral judgements and decisions in the everyday business of life, of the form 'What ought I to do now?' 'Was he justified in doing that?' 'Would it be honest to say that?' etc. What goes on at this level provides the subject matter for moral reflection at the two higher levels. On the next storey are 'wise men' who seek to develop consistent and defensible moral theories through the examination and criticism of the plain man's judgements. This activity is sometimes called 'normative ethics'. Historically it has generally been undertaken by philosophers who have operated both on this floor and on the one above. On this latter, the top storey, are philosophers regularly engaged in what is the characteristic task of philosophy (and, in the view of some analytic philosophers, its only task) that of analysing the concepts and the arguments of those who are operating on the two lower floors. They are engaged, that is to say, in 'meta-ethical' enquiry, raising such questions as: 'What is the logical character of moral arguments?; Are they characteristically deductive or inductive or of some other kind?; Are moral judgements subjective or objective?; Does morality require to be justified?; Or must any attempted justification be circular?'

It has often been thought that 'meta-ethics' is entirely independent of what happens at the other two stages, in the sense that a particular meta-ethical theory does not entail or have any other bearing, from a logical point of view, upon particular moral theories or moral judgements. The purpose of philosophy is purely clarificatory. Hence traditional philosophers such as Plato, Aristotle, Butler, Kant, who embarked upon philosophical enquiry with a view to discovering how we ought to act, are thought to have made a serious blunder.

But this view of the relationship between moral philosophy and morality, or between 'meta-ethics' and 'normative ethics', this doctrine that 'philosophy is neutral', fits some conceptions of morality very much better than others and itself reflects a particular metaphysical position, as Iris Murdoch saw clearly in her essay on 'Vision and Choice in Morality'. It goes well with an intuitionist theory of the sort put forward by Moore and Ross. For if there is a 'common moral consciousness', as they believed, the task of moral theory (at the second level) will be to systematize it, so far as possible; and the test of a moral theory will, of course, be its capacity to accommodate our moral intuitions. Moral philosophers (at the third level) may reflect upon the definition of moral words, whether they can be defined in terms of non-moral words, whether 'right' can be defined in terms of 'good' etc., but they cannot call in question the deliverances of the common moral consciousness. It also consorts well with subjectivism, for moral philosophers, on that view, can classify the various uses to which moral expressions are put in everyday usage; they can distinguish between the evaluative and descriptive use of language, but they are in no position to pronounce, *qua* philosophers, upon the acceptability of the moral judgements that are actually made.

It suits a utilitarian very much less, or at any rate the sort of utilitarian I have characterized as the scientific humanist. No doubt it is possible for a utilitarian to be, like Smart, a subjectivist; he just favours generalized benevolence and hopes that other people, once they understand the issues, will feel as he does. Other people may, however, feel differently and, if they do, Smart cannot show them to be wrong—or, indeed, hold them to be wrong in any strong sense. But this is an uncharacteristic posture for a utilitarian. More commonly he is a moral objectivist who believes that the entire institution of morality exists to harmonize human purposes so that people can together achieve happiness in a society. Hence he must believe that anyone who rejects utilitarianism fails to understand what morality is, because he fails to appreciate its point and purpose. The utilitarian, *qua philosopher,* is committed to this moral theory; and, if the common moral consciousness cannot be squared with it, 'so much the worse for the common moral consciousness',[4] which the utilitarian philosopher suspects in any case to have been influenced by traditional ways of thought or by some philosophically suspect system of religious ethics. And these traditional theories, for their part, tend to resemble scientific humanism in basing morality upon, or at least relating it to, pervasive features of human life. So the doctrine that philosophy is neutral—that activities on the third level are logically independent of what goes on at the other two—is itself not neutral and cannot, I believe, be sustained; it begs the question against many familiar ways of thinking about morality, in which, as Iris Murdoch puts it, 'moral concepts are regarded as deep moral configurations of the world, rather than as lines drawn round separate factual areas.'[5]

[4] As J. J. C. Smart says, *Utilitarianism For and Against,* p. 68.

[5] Quoted on p. 68 above.

Nevertheless the model has its usefulness, so long as the levels are not thought of as independent. In terms of it we can distinguish the different sorts of disagreement that there are about morality. Thus (on the ground floor), people disagree about what ought to be done in particualr situations and about what moral principles to appeal to; they disagree also as to the moral vocabulary to be employed; so that not only do they give different answers to the same questions, but they often insist on asking different questions. And when we inquire further we find that these differences relate to differences on the middle storey, differences as to the kind of moral system they are operating with. Thus 'Should this boy be punished?' might receive the answer 'Yes' from one teacher, 'No' from another, where they, nevertheless, agree as to what the boy has done and in what circumstances. They mean the same thing by 'punishment' and they disagree only in their judgement of the particular case. But another teacher might not want to use the term 'punish' at all as having undesirably retributive associations; he would prefer to ask 'Does this boy need special treatment?' Similarly the writer of an agony column may assure a correspondent who is unfaithful to his wife that he should not feel guilty about it, not because guilt is inappropriate in this case, although it might have been appropriate in another, but because she feels that guilt is a pathological condition which is always to be avoided. She has no use for the concept. We are now so inured to this phenomenon that I can remember the shock of surprise—and I am bound to add, pleasure—when a local psychiatrist, to whom a pupil of mine had been referred with work problems, reported: 'I think the trouble is that this man is lazy.' I had not expected this word to be in his vocabulary.

Still further differences may arise as to the correct interpretation or analysis of this state of affairs, differences this time on the top storey. A subjectivist philosopher will maintain that the difference is to be understood as a difference in evaluation. Although the two teachers use different words, which create the impression that they see the world differently, the truth is that one could take the words used by each and separate out the evaluative and descriptive components in them. Once this is done the argument between them can be clearly presented as being about what descriptive states of affairs each is prepared individually to commend or condemn. But another philosopher may complain that this account seriously distorts the character of morality and moral discourse, and gives an entirely misleading impression of the way morality is related to our total understanding of man and the world. These two philosophers will differ profoundly as to what morality *is,* and it is likely that their difference will, so to speak, make itself felt all the way down the line, at every level of discussion. It is this phenomenon which accounts for the profound unsatisfactoriness of almost all debates on television. The participants do not have the time to explore, or even to acknowledge the deeper disagreements which underlie their differing vocabularies and patterns of argument. So they consistently talk past one another. Thus the attempt, which is characteristic of liberal humanism in all its forms, to distinguish ideals from some basic type of morality and to keep them separate, while at the same time insisting that only the basic morality is open to rational discussion, makes it difficult for an opponent to state a reasoned case against it. For such a case is liable to be dismissed as the expression of an ideal and, as such, not to be reasoned about; and the proponent of it is likely to be classified as a 'fanatic', who is prepared to subordinate other people's interests and his own to an ideal. Many who have been impressed by the power of Hare's argument, in the fully developed form in which it appears in *Freedom and Reason,* and who have nevertheless failed to be wholly convinced, are acutely aware of this difficulty. To be prepared to allow ideals to override interests, one's own included, does indeed seem to merit the epithet 'fanatical', but it has to be kept in mind that it is only in Hare's terms that this is an appropriate description of what Hare's opponent is doing. For in Hare's terms an individual's interests are defined as what he wants, or is likely to want, etc., and the opponent is maintaining that interests in this sense should sometimes be overridden. But this is not the sense in which the opponent is himself using the word 'interest'. He employs it in a sense which is closer to common usage, according to which it makes perfectly good sense to say that a man may want (or be likely to want etc.) what is not in his own interest. Of course he will agree that men normally want what they think is in their own interest and, indeed, very often what actually is in their own interest; and that it is normally in their interest to get what they want. But not always, and not by definition. The difference between the two standpoints is specially clear in relation to the education of children. It follows from Hare's view that parents may be said to have brought up their child in accordance with the child's interest only if the child later thanks them for it, or would thank them for it given adequate information. We may agree that this is normally a good test, but not, surely, invariably. A child may be brought up to be conventional and complacent and subsequently thank his parents for helping to make him the paragon he believes himself to be. Or he may be brought up to be restless and sceptical, and criticize his parents for having helped to make him so; how much easier life would have been if he were not! Must we be prepared to say that the first man is better off because he is more contented, or the second man worse off because he is less contented? Of course, we think it wrong to *condition* people or otherwise mould them into conformity with our ideal, but this is likely to be because our ideal of human excellence (or at any rate a large part of it), is one of independent, autonomous persons; and, if someone does not want to be independent and autonomous we shall, as parents or educators, feel bound to do our best to make him so, whether or not we think that he will eventually thank us for our pains.

Thus Hare is right in holding that such a conception of 'interest' is related to an ideal of human nature, in terms of which what the individual wants may properly be subordinated to something that is believed to matter more. But, equally, Hare's definition of 'interest', and the uses he puts it to, reflect a particular sort of liberal ideal, according to which what the individual wants should not be overridden in this way. To make this point is not to stigmatize Hare's moral theory as in any way improper or unfair. For the critic believes, as Hare does not, that ideals are open to rational argument. He does not deny that Hare has produced a powerful case for his type of liberalism (much of which will need to be incorporated in any adequate moral theory). He simply argues that a central feature of it, his treatment of interests and ideals and their relationship, is open to challenge and in need of further defence.

Hare anticipates this response. He supposes an opponent to say: 'I am not going to be either a fanatic or a liberal; I am simply going to stop using your concepts',[6] and claims to have a decisive answer. For his own account is, he claims, more *general* than that of his opponent: 'We can get the better of our present attacker because our language is general enough to express any dispute which he may say he is having with us.' But precisely the same claim can be made by his opponent, as the present discussion illustrates.

This situation lands us in a familiar predicament. There seems no hope of providing a philosophical account of morality or of moral language which will be entirely neutral, which does not favour certain systems of normative morality as against others, certain conceptions of the meaning of life as against others. And it is tempting to conclude that nothing is left but for each side to develop its own total position as coherently as it can and then to hope that it will prove psychologically persuasive. For, it is tempting to suppose, all rational resources have, *ex hypothesi*, been exhausted. This is what Hare recommends in a well known passage, part of which I quoted earlier:

> . . . If pressed to justify a decision completely, we have to give a complete specification of the way of life of which it is a part. This complete specification it is impossible in practice to give; the nearest attempts are those given by the great religions, especially those which can point to historical persons who carried out the way of life in practice. Suppose, however, that we can give it. If the inquirer still goes on asking 'But why *should* I live like that?' then there is no further answer to give him, because we have already, *ex hypothesi*, said everything that could be included in this further answer. We can only ask him to make up his own mind which way he ought to live; for in the end everything rests upon such a decision of principle. He has to decide whether to accept that way of life or not; if he accepts it, then we can proceed to justify the decisions that are based upon it; if he does not accept it, then let him accept some other, and try to live by it. The sting is in the last clause. To describe such ultimate decisions as arbitrary, because *ex hypothesi* everything which could be used to justify them has already been included in the decision, would be like saying that a complete description of the universe was utterly unfounded because no further

[6] *Freedom and Reason*, pp. 200–2.

fact could be called upon in corroboration of it. This is not how we use the words 'arbitrary' and 'unfounded'. Far from being arbitrary, such a decision would be the most well-founded of decisions, because it would be based upon a consideration of everything upon which it could possibly be founded.[7]

I am sure that Hare is right in stressing that in order to justify a decision completely we have to relate it to the way of life of which it is a part and in pointing to the great religions as the nearest approaches to this in practice, but I do not think that he entirely escapes the charge of arbitrariness. His failure to do so is associated with a way of looking at the situation which comes out clearly in this passage. A way of life, as Hare conceives it, seems to be a complex set of decisions taken in the face of a world which can be exhaustively described in terms which are metaphysically neutral. This world, which is entirely devoid of theoretical content, is confronted by agents who can freely determine the attitudes they shall adopt towards it, the choices they shall make within it. This picture of an unencumbered will confronting an unmysterious world is itself an interpretation of the human situation rather than a bare description of it. As such it represents, as Iris Murdoch clearly sees, a very particular vision of the nature of the world and the place of morality in it.

But what alternative is there to Hare's programme? I suggest that, when faced by these conflicting systems, we are not reduced to sheer confrontation. Not only can we examine their internal consistency and coherence, we can consider how well they cohere with what is scientifically supported and with our general knowledge of human nature. We can test them against our own moral insights and those of people we trust; and, if this is stigmatized as arguing in a circle, we can consider, also, what grounds there may be, in the systems under review, for paying attention to people's moral intuitions. And, finally, we can see how adequately they are able to account for one another. Serious and thoughtful men, it is reasonable to suppose, reflecting on what they hold to be of overriding importance in human life, are not likely to be wholly mistaken; and if we wish to regard them as mistaken, in any particular respect, our contention will be reinforced if

[7] *The Language of Morals,* p. 69.

we can explain intelligibly how they might have been misled. In the process we may sometimes be compelled to have recourse to psychological, sociological or even straightforwardly historical explanations of why men think as they do, but if we avail ourselves of this licence too readily or too frequently, we shall be in danger of exposing our own position to similar attack.[8]

I have called attention to a certain dissatisfaction among reflective persons with some of the most characteristic moral attitudes of the times, and I have been suggesting that this might be allayed by a specifically Christian ethic deriving from a specifically Christian metaphysic; and that there is much in the way that discontent is voiced which supports this view. The entire phenomenon could, perhaps, be explained as no more than a powerful nostalgia for the Christian past. Are not these thinkers hankering for a morality that can no longer be had in anything like the old form or on anything like the old terms? The answer to these questions depends on the extent to which it is possible to construct a religious ethic which can survive the kind of tests outlined above.

[8] I have discussed the problem of rational choice between rival world-views in *The Justification of Religious Belief,* Macmillan (1973), especially chapter 5.

8

The Theological Frontier of Ethics

The task before us is to provide a defence for the traditional conscience. What is needed is an understanding of morality which is capable of being defended at each of the three levels at which moral disputes take place and which can explain how it is that moral considerations have an integrity of their own while yet being open, as they plainly are, to the influence of divergent world-views. These requirements would be met if morality were thought of as essentially concerned with the fulfilment of men's needs as individuals and as members of society—with the necessary conditions of human well-being. There is disagreement, but not unlimited disagreement, as to what these needs are, for some human needs are so obvious and exigent that it is virtually impossible to overlook them—hence the widespread acceptance of moral platitudes—while others are more or less controversial, depending for their recognition on truths (or alleged truths) about human nature which are open to dispute among adherents of different world-views. Science, especially the psychological and social sciences, may well extend and deepen our understanding of human needs, so that the scientific humanist would not from this standpoint be wholly mistaken. His error would lie chiefly in his dogmatic insistence on regarding science as the sole accredited source of knowledge of human nature. And morality would have a point which all could appreciate.

If morality is conceived of in this way, it becomes easier to chart 'the theological frontier of ethics'. For Christianity has its own characteristic conception of human needs; the needs of men are those of a creature whom God loves, has created, redeemed and destined for eternal life, and who, therefore, has an unconditional value. The moral law is not simply the arbitrary command of God, but is based upon the nature of man as God made him. And God does not make just rational beings whose entire duty is to exemplify a universal pattern, as rational humanists have always tended to suppose, but individual persons with their own particular vocations, and their own access to the means of grace. So that there is a place also for the characteristically romantic values of spontaneity and authenticity.

I want, in the remainder of this book, to develop this theme and to show how this conception of morality can provide a secure and intelligible basis for the demands of the traditional conscience. But this can only be done if the underlying philosophical thesis is defensible. What I have been expounding in this preliminary and tentative fashion could be described as a form of theological naturalism and, as such, it is open to all the criticisms that have been directed against naturalism in ethics. At this point my resolve to adhere to Lord Gifford's injunction that these lectures should be 'popular' is liable to come under some strain. For it is impossible to avoid a certain amount of technical moral philosophy. In discussing Hare's version of liberal humanism and in complaining that he fails to appreciate the extent to which moral attitudes and moral theories (his own included) tend to reflect divergent world-views I have so far dodged his very acute criticism of any attempt to derive moral judgements from statements of fact, whether of empirical or metaphysical fact.

As we have seen, Hare bases his critique upon an analysis of language. In the case of a word like 'good' it is necessary to distinguish between the meaning of the word 'good' which is given by its use as a term of commendation, i.e. its 'evaluative meaning'; and the criteria for its application, which will consist in those characteristics in virtue of which the speaker resolves to commend the action, character or situation; its 'descriptive meaning'. The criteria specified will vary with the moral code of the agent; the commendatory function of the word remains constant. A request for reasons for calling something good is to be met by indicating the characteristics in virtue of which we hold it to be good. Similarly with decisions. If called upon to justify a decision I must refer to the principle upon which it was based; and, if called upon to justify that, I must indicate the consequences of the universal application of the principle (for it is these which give content to the principle). And so, as Hare points out, we could eventually be driven back to a complete specification of the way of life of which the original principle is a part.

Thus Hare admits the relevance of world-views to morality, but insists that at each stage it is the free decision of the individual to pick out certain characteristics rather than others as objects of commendation which gives these the status of 'reasons'. The agent could always choose otherwise and, if he did, he would, in so choosing, have adopted other reasons. The only constraint upon him is that of consistency. He must be prepared to accept the consequences of any choice he makes.

There is something distinctly odd about this notion of choosing what shall count as a reason,[1] but Hare is prepared to accept this and other paradoxes in order to secure a single objective, which is to account for the 'action-guiding' function of moral language:

> [All value-words] have it as their distinctive function either to commend or in some other way to guide choices or actions; and it is this essential feature which defies any analysis in purely factual terms. But to guide choices or actions, a moral judgement has to be such that, if a person assents to it, he must assent to some imperative sentence derivable from it.[2]

Hare maintains that in order to know how to use a 'descriptive' word, we should have to know 'to what kinds of things it was properly applied' and no more; whereas evaluative words have in addition 'prescriptive meaning'. Thus if 'good' were to be thought of as being simply a descriptive word, there would have to be a meaning-rule which says that the word is applicable to a certain kind of man; if it is thought of as also having prescriptive meaning, anyone who learns it will be learning not merely to use a word in a certain way but to commend or prescribe for imitation a certain sort of man.

It is worth noticing in the first place that this very simple dichotomy leaves us uncertain how to classify a great deal of our vocabulary. Many words that we commonly use involve some sort of judgement or assessment on our part for their correct application, e.g., aesthetic judgement in the case of 'subtle' or 'harmonious', historical or political judgement in the case of 'revolutionary' or 'influential'. The terms I have

[1] Cf. G. J. Warnock, *Contemporary Moral Philosophy*, Macmillan (1967), pp. 46–7.

[2] *The Language of Morals*, p. 171.

constantly employed in this book, 'romantic', 'rational', 'liberal' come naturally to mind. It would be quite unplausible to suggest that there are rules of language which determine uniquely how they should be applied. When one has achieved mastery of the English language, it is a separate task to learn to think historically or philosophically. Thus any educated Englishman knows the meaning of the word 'revolutionary'; it may take a trained historian or student of politics to determine whether, in the light of certain evidence, a revolutionary situation existed. Yet it is equally clear that these judgements need not be prescriptive. The historian may or may not take an attitude to the facts or prescribe a certain type of behaviour for imitation. Moreover, if he does use such words predominantly to commend or condemn, as he very possibly may, he does not have complete freedom as to the sense he shall give them. Although there are not fixed rules of language which determine their application, the criteria for their use are very much more restricted than for the use of very general words like 'good' and 'bad'. You cannot choose to call *anything* brilliant, subtle, or harmonious any more than you can call *anyone* just, merciful, or courageous.

Nevertheless Hare will insist on two points. The first is that 'good' at any rate, as the most general word of commendation, is independent of criteria, at least when used in a fully evaluative sense, and must be independent, if it is to exercise the function of guiding choices. The second is that, unless this point is appreciated, one cannot understand how our more specific moral vocabulary is open to criticism and capable of change and development. But, as critics of Hare have pointed out, there is a close relationship between the use of 'good' and of these other more specific expressions. Suppose I am asked my opinion of a philosophical work. I say that I find it obscure, dull, involved, lacking in logical rigour, pretentious, and incoherent. Does if make any sort of sense if I then pronounce it a good book, asserting my logical right to apply what criteria I like to the evaluation of philosophical works? To be sure it can still be a good book, if, in spite of this accumulation of vices, it has countervailing virtues, but if I close the list there it would seem that I am no longer free to praise it (or perhaps we ought to say, not that I cannot praise it, but that I cannot reasonably praise it). The only way in which Hare can take care of this sort of example, so far as I can see, is to regard 'philosophical work' as a functional expression; so that 'good philosophical work', makes clear the criteria to be employed, just as 'good auger' or 'good hammer' does; but philosophy does not have a function in any relevant sense. Competent judges may differ as to what are the requirements for good philosophy, and as to whether a particular work satisfies them, but implicit in their judgement is a readiness to produce reasons which are defensible.

I do not myself think that the moral case is fundamentally different. For example, I do not see how I can reasonably call a man good because he is a coward. Of course I can commend him if, in spite of or perhaps even because of being a coward, he has developed certain virtues. He may have been forced by constant humiliations to recognize his own weakness and so have attained an honesty and humility denied to many stronger men (though honesty and humility require courage of a sort). But I cannot (or cannot reasonably) commend him for his cowardice as such if it is to be *moral* commendation.

The prescriptivist answer to this is to remind us that 'cowardice' is itself a value word, or normally used as such, and that, in so far as I cannot praise a man for cowardice, it is because in doing so I should involve myself in a sort of evaluative contradiction, commending and condemning someone on account of the same characteristics in one and the same breath. The very language I use has valuations built into it, which I cannot remove at will. In Hare's phrase, it 'incapsulates the standards of the society'.[3] But, it will be said, I can explicitly dissociate myself from these standards; I can commend him on account of those neutral characteristics which are the ground for his being commonly condemned. I can praise him, if I choose, for running away in battle, telling lies rather than endure discomfort, agreeing with everyone for fear of giving offence, etc. I can list the characteristics commonly associated with cowardice and resolve to commend them.

So it is said. But if anyone actually took this line (in life, not in philosophical discussion) we should, surely, in this case also, want his reasons for commending the man. We should

[3] *Freedom and Reason*, p. 25.

want to know the point or purpose of his cowardly behaviour, whom it purported to benefit and in what way; and if the speaker answered simply by developing in further detail the sort of behaviour he wanted us to approve—elaborating, so to say, the cowardly way of life—we should simply be non-plussed. We should not say, as the prescriptivist supposes we should, 'Here is a man with a somewhat eccentric set of moral standards!' We should say, I imagine, that he appeared to have no moral sense at all.

'We should, no doubt, react in this way,' the prescriptivist might reply, 'but does this settle the argument? Is it not too short a way with prescriptivism to refer to what "we" should or should not say?' The prescriptivist suspects that such a move is no more than a covert appeal to the traditional standards which have been 'incapsulated' in 'our' language. To allow this appeal is, he believes, effectively to rule out the possibility of criticizing these standards. And this is, without doubt, a justified complaint against some formulations of 'naturalism'. Thus Hare says:

It is useful to have in our language both secondarily evaluative words like 'industrious' and primarily evaluative words like 'good'; and we should therefore be suspicious, if any philosopher seeks to persuade us in the interest of concreteness to neglect the study of words like 'good' and concentrate on words like 'industrious' and 'courageous'. The object of such a manoeuvre might be to convince us that *all* moral words have their descriptive meaning irremovably attached to them; but, fortunately for the usefulness of moral language in expressing changing standards, this is not so. To take this line would be to give an account of moral language which is, so far as it goes, true, but not sufficiently general (in the sense in which Newtonian mechanics is not sufficiently general). The account would suffice for the moral language of an irrevocably closed society, in which a change of moral standards was unthinkable; but it does not do justice to the moral language of a society like our own, in which some people sometimes think about ultimate moral questions, and in which, therefore, morality changes.[4]

That the meaning of moral words may change and that people's views about morality may change, and that existing standards are always, in principle, open to criticism, these are facts to which the prescriptivist constantly, and rightly, calls attention. This is surely a conclusive reason for rejecting the sort of naturalism (called by Hare 'descriptivism') which holds

[4] *Freedom and Reason*, p. 25.

that the inference from a non-moral description of something to a moral conclusion about it is *an inference whose validity is due solely to the meaning of the words in it.*[5] Against such a view Hare insists that 'in saying that it is proper to call a certain kind of man "good" (for example a man who feeds his children, does not beat his wife, etc.) we are not just explaining the meaning of a word; it is not mere verbal instruction that we are giving, but something more: moral instruction'.[6]

In this he is clearly right. If someone wishes to state a case for the practice of wife-beating, which has been entirely respectable in some societies, (including our own in previous centuries), it is not enough to tell him that non-wife-beating is part of the *definition* of 'good' as applied to men. The question at issue is, however, whether it at all follows from this that 'moral instruction' is what Hare and other prescriptivists take it to be. Does it, in particular, follow that 'moral instruction' cannot be criticized or defended on objective grounds e.g. by reference, as Hampshire suggests, to the natural, or the supernatural order? In other words, is a philosopher who wishes to state a case for the objectivity of moral judgements committed to the view, which Hare identifies with naturalism, that 'in saying that it is proper to call a certain kind of man "good" . . . we are just explaining the meaning of a word'?

It is not at all obvious that he is. In recent moral philosophy it has too easily been assumed that the choice lies between a 'flat' naturalism and a 'sharp' non-naturalism. The 'flat' naturalist maintains that inferences from 'is' to 'ought' are possible by way of meaning-rules alone. The 'sharp' non-naturalist denies this and asserts as a counter thesis the typical prescriptivist argument that, as a matter of logic, no imperative conclusion can be drawn from premisses which do not contain at least one imperative. All argument against either one of these positions is taken to be *pro tanto* an argument for the other, since no account is taken of any but strictly deductive inferences; although, in appraising intellectual as well as moral qualities, we are familiar with terms of assessment, like 'reasonable' and 'implausible', which require to be supported by reasons, but cannot be defined by reference to any list of determinate properties.

[5] *Freedom and Reason*, p. 21, my italics.

[6] *Freedom and Reason*, p. 23.

In talking earlier about cowardice, I was unsure whether to say that you could not call a man 'good' on account of cowardice or that you could not *reasonably* do so. I was tempted to say 'you cannot commend cowardice' on the ground that it does not make sense to say 'cowardice is good', so, that if someone went through the motions of commending cowardice, we should not understand what he meant. Part of the problem here is that the conditions in which we are prepared to say we understand what someone means are elastic. In the present case of someone who said 'cowardice is good' we should have no difficulty in surmising that he was in favour of cowardice and prepared to recommend cowardice to others. If, in reply to questioning, he insisted that by 'good' he meant 'morally good' it would be less easy to see what he meant, because it would be hard to envisage the form which a moral defence of cowardice might take. Still we might understand him as believing that such a defence was possible. If, however, we insisted against him that there is a *rule of language* in virtue of which 'cowardice is morally good' does not make sense, he might very reasonably feel that we had cut off the debate in a somewhat arbitrary fashion. If what he says is nonsense, it is not merely verbal nonsense, but moral nonsense, and it is because it is generally agreed to be moral nonsense that it is tempting to regard it as verbal nonsense too, so completely has this particular standard been incapsulated in our language. Indeed it may be the case, as I think it is, that the status of courage as a virtue is so secure that there is no language that does not incapsulate it, so that we could argue with some plausibility that to deny it involves a contradiction in terms. But even this does not mean that all criticism of the incapsulated standard is ruled out and the appeal to language alone settles the argument definitively. It means only that criticism in fact fails. No one has produced and perhaps no one can produce good moral reasons for rejecting this particular standard and for altering our language accordingly.

I have deliberately chosen an example in which the moral arguments appear to be conclusive and in which, therefore, the prescriptivist case has least plausibility. What are we to say about the more controversial cases in relation to which prescriptivism is intuitively far more convincing? Some of

Hare's most illuminating passages describe the way in which a word's evaluative meaning may alter, while its descriptive meaning remains the same, or vice versa; how with some words the evaluative meaning is primary, in others the descriptive. An example of the way in which a word which used to be morally neutral may come, on the lips of certain people, to be a term of moral commendation, is the word 'adult'. For most people it still refers simply to a stage in the biological development of the human individual and has little or no moral significance; they assume that, from a moral point of view, adults are as likely to be bad as good. It has purely 'descriptive' meaning. But, for some people, to be 'adult' is to display a certain range of approved attitudes, and we know well enough what these are likely to be. An 'adult' person is one who is morally autonomous, progressive in politics, and has liberal ideas about sex. One could scarcely call Mrs Mary Whitehouse 'adult'. It would, surely, be absurd to criticize this usage on the ground that the word 'adult' simply does not *mean* this. That would be to place a purely linguistic ban on a putative advance in moral awareness. As Hare remarks, 'to say that in all moral words the descriptive meaning is primary would be suitable to the moral language of a closed society.' Nevertheless the new usage may reasonably be asked to show its credentials for reception into our moral vocabulary. The mere fact that a number of people employ the word 'adult' as a term of approval is not enough to constitute it a term of moral commendation though it may be enough to constitute it a term of approval (cf. 'professional'). Before we can understand it as such we shall need to know what it is about being adult that is thought to be morally good and why. In point of fact we shall discover that this usage reflects an ideal, and this ideal is bound up more or less explicitly with a theory about the relationship between the psychological and the moral development of the individual, as observed in Western European society, and the theory determines the selection of qualities that are thought of as being characteristically adult. The ideal and the theory that goes with it is, in fact, related to a particular world-view; a variety of scientific humanism of the sort sponsored by Alex Comfort. Given the theory it is plausible to hold that in virtue of a meaning-rule anyone having these characteristics is adult and worthy of moral commendation; and, when we understand the theory, we can understand the usage, although we are not bound to accept it, unless we accept the theory. The theory is controversial; it can be criticized and it can be defended, but for neither criticism nor defence is it enough simply to opt for or against the qualities of character which the theory selects for approbation. We have to assess the merits of the opposing world-views. Because of the role of theory in the selection of qualities for approbation or disapprobation, it must be comparatively rare for precisely the same qualities to be approved by one party and, quite independently, disapproved by another. For instance, when Hume condemned 'the whole train of monkish virtues' the traits which he was attacking had been picked out for him by the moral theory implicit in monasticism and he was predisposed to condemn them by his total lack of sympathy with the ideals of monasticism. It is most improbable that, if Hume had never encountered the monastic tradition, he should have formed a con-attitude to just those traits of character, which were the objects of a pro-attitude on the part of St. Benedict.

Thus we can see that the language we use and the theories it presupposes may undergo change and be open to criticism of different sorts, including moral criticism, without being 'evaluative' as understood by the prescriptivist; that is, without the individual speaker being logically committed by his use of the language to behaving in certain ways, or making certain choices.

So also with cowardice. I can, of course, express myself as in favour of cowardice and resolve to live in a cowardly fashion. I can explicitly dissociate myself from the use of any language in which traditional approbation of courage is incapsulated. It does not, however, follow that in so doing I am taking a moral stand. Whether that is so depends on whether courage actually is a moral virtue, as traditionally believed, or whether, as I am now supposedly maintaining, cowardice is. Nothing in the argument has any tendency to show that there could not be reasons, even conclusive reasons of, a moral kind for the one position or the other (but not, of course, for both).

But, it will be objected, if this point were conceded, the word 'good' would have lost its function of guiding choices.

There would no longer be any logical connection between my recognition that an action was good, and my choosing it. It would be perfectly reasonable for me to say 'It's good; so what?' Unless in calling an action cowardly, and so bad, I commit myself to not doing actions of this sort; unless, that is, I am using the words 'cowardly' and 'bad' in a fully evaluative sense as the prescriptivist understands it, there is an unbridgeable gap of a logical sort between my use of such moral language and my conduct. But clearly the whole point of moral language is to guide conduct.

This objection is at the heart of the prescriptivist case and it requires an answer. Quite obviously if a man says 'X is wrong', yet his conduct in respect of X is to all appearance precisely what it would have been had he not expressed this opinion, there is something amiss. Is he insincere or morally weak, or is it possible that he is morally defective and unable to understand the meaning of the word 'wrong'? The prescriptivist says that the trouble is that he doesn't sincerely assent to the imperative: 'Let me not do X', and so isn't using 'wrong' in its evaluative sense; for, if he were using it in its evaluative sense, he would refrain from doing X. On this view the possible alternatives are merged in one—a sort of insincerity. And, as has often been pointed out, this has the paradoxical consequence that it is logically impossible not to do those things which we think we ought to do, or to do those things which we think we ought not to do (so long as 'ought' is used in a fully evaluative sense).

Hare[7] displays great ingenuity and genuine insight in trying to mitigate this paradox, but even if it can be done, which I doubt, it remains very much open to question whether prescriptivism does, in any case, account itself for the action-guiding function of moral words. There is an ambiguity in the conception of guiding action. We could say that beliefs guide our action in so far as they provide reasons for acting in a certain way, or in so far as they supply motives for acting in a certain way. I do not myself see how the prescriptivist analysis of moral judgements shows them to be action-guiding in either sense. For, if we ask what on this view is the reason for doing what we ought to do, we are told that it is that in

[7] See especially *Freedom and Reason*, chapter V, 'Backsliding'.

using the expression 'I ought to do X' we have expressed the intention of so doing; but this provides no reason for forming one intention rather than another. And if we ask what motive is provided for doing what we ought to do, we are told that the motive is that we have formed the intention of doing it, but no explanation is offered why we form this sort of intention (moral intention) at all.

But the prescriptivist is right to press his question: How *do* moral judgements guide action? And if we reject his answer we must look for another. We must consider how morality can provide reasons for action and also appropriate motives for it.

If we regard the concept of morality as logically bound up with people's needs and interests it becomes possible to do justice to these requirements, while at the same time avoiding both the 'naturalistic fallacy' and the 'prescriptivist paradox'. Moral words will have (to use Stephen Toulmin's expression)[8] a 'gerundive' force in virtue of which they cannot be defined in terms of expressions which lack this force. What Hare and others say about evaluative meaning can be applied *mutatis mutandis* to this gerundive force. To use 'industrious' or 'adult' evaluatively in this sense is to use it in such a way as to imply that the characteristics in virtue of which a person is said to be industrious or adult are such as to make him worthy or 'meet' to be imitated: which in turn implies that reasons of the appropriate kind could be given for the assessment. If the reasons are to be moral reasons, they must relate to some intelligible conception of human well-being. It is possible to call someone industrious in an evaluative sense in this way, i.e. in such a way as to imply that he is worth imitating, without actually imitating him or even intending to do so. In that case, no doubt, the speaker could be regarded as a hypocrite but not as failing to make a moral judgement at all.

On this view what a man commits himself to when he asserts that an action is wrong, or uses another form of words that implies it, is that there are sufficient reasons of a moral kind for not doing it, and these reasons can perfectly well be objective. To ask, 'Why shouldn't I do what is wrong?', which for

[8] See *The Place of Reason in Ethics*, Cambridge University Press (1950), pp. 70–2.

the prescriptivist is a nonsense question, amounts to asking, 'Why shouldn't I do what there are sufficient reasons of a moral kind for not doing?' This is a nonsense question if what are looked for are moral reasons, but is perfectly intelligible if what is looked for is a justification of morality.

To adopt this idea of morality is to side finally with those who take morality to be constituted by the sort of considerations that count in favour of a moral judgement as against those who define a man's morality as consisting of the set of principles that he regards as overriding. So Heliogabalus must be described as choosing to live his life by aesthetic rather than moral principles because he thought interesting colour contrasts mattered more than men's lives. From a moral point of view moral principles ought to be overriding, but in fact they sometimes are not. This should not worry those who are accustomed to confess, 'We have left undone those things which we ought to have done; and we have done those things which we ought not to have done'.

What I have sketched is simply a basic framework of morality. Any developed morality is a much more complex matter, but I am suggesting that the complications are systematically connected with the needs of men in their varied social and personal relationships. No first order morality is adequate which does not reflect these; and no philosophical account of morality is satisfactory which does not recognize them. As soon, however, as one has got beyond the barest necessities for any kind of human life, and the very basic morality that is demanded by them, one emerges into an area of possible controversy. Moralists differ, often as a matter of temperament, as to whether to emphasize the moral claims that derive from institutions as they are, 'incapsulated' in the language of custom and tradition, or whether to stress the moral criticism of the *status quo.* But although existing institutions are always in principle open to criticism and the current language similarly open to revision, as the prescriptivist rightly stresses, such criticism and such revision must, to be moral at all, relate to some conception of human nature and its possibilities.

In the light of these considerations we can also make sense of the confusion in morals and in moral philosophy which I attempted to illustrate in my opening chapter. I remarked about the writers of my imaginary letters to *The Times,* that 'these writers are divided not only in their opinions but in their vocabulary. They inhabit different words of discourse'. That is to say, they express different moral viewpoints related to different conceptions of human well-being. These, to use Strawson's language, are based upon varied, and often conflicting, 'pictures of man' which in turn reflect different 'profound general statements about man and the universe'. Christianity is one of these and, as such, has its own characteristic conception of the nature and scope of morality and of its place in human life.

If, then, we are looking for a system of normative ethics which we can wholeheartedly accept, it must be one whose rationale we can also understand and accept, and which makes sense both of our deepest moral convictions—what I have been calling our 'intuitions'—and of what we have reason to believe about man and the universe. If it is among our deepest moral convictions that morality is objective and categorical, and that moral principles are overriding, it must do justice to this fact. If we are persuaded that there are moral principles which hold, irrespective of consequences, or which can be set aside on account of consequences only in exceptional circumstances, it must take account of this too. But it must, also, be able to justify this procedure—to explain why it is that we should trust these profound convictions of ours and not dismiss them as mere irrational prejudices, however deeply held. Indeed, it must do more than this; it must account for the fact that morality has an integrity and autonomy of its own, so that we may properly reject a total view of life because its ethical implications are unacceptable. This is what is involved in the vindication of what I have called 'the traditional conscience'. Of course there is another alternative altogether open to modern man. He may abandon the traditional conscience and rejoice with Nietzsche in his consequent liberation. But my argument is addressed to those who are not prepared to accept that alternative. So, while leaving open the possibility, as I am bound to do, that an entirely secular world-view might provide the traditional conscience with the rationale it needs (although I do not know of one that does) I want now in what remains of this book to consider, in relation to Christian theism, the following questions:

(i) Does it show reason why certain moral principles should be given more weight than they merit on purely utilitarian grounds?

(ii) Does it offer a justification for morality?

(iii) Does it do justice to the extent to which morality is autonomous?

(iv) Does it provide a rationale for, and a critique of, moral intuitions?

9

The Dilemma Illustrated: The Sanctity of Life

The first question is best answered in relation to particular examples, and the obvious one to take first is the one selected by Hampshire, respect for human life. Hampshire uses the expression 'sanctity of human life' and asks how its use can be justified: 'The question cannot be evaded: what is the rational basis for acting as if human life has a peculiar value, quite beyond the value of any other natural things . . .?'[1] That it has such a peculiar value is certainly one of the clearest intuitions of all who have been reared in the cultural traditions of the West (though there is now less agreement than there used to be as to its practical implications and a general disinclination to inquire into its rationale). There are, of course, good utilitarian reasons for the existence in all societies of a general prohibition upon taking life, since a society which lacked this restriction would be unlikely to survive for long. So it finds its place in Strawson's 'basic social morality' and Hart's 'minimum content of natural law'. But this sort of justification is compatible with attitudes and practices which must be abhorrent to any sensitive conscience. Societies have survived which treated the lives of foreigners as of comparatively little account, and slavery as an institution has flourished throughout the centuries. To kill the weak and the old may even promote survival. Indeed the very emphasis upon the preservation of society as a reason for respecting human life can easily result in subordinating the individual's life to the interests of society where this is thought to be necessary. Sir Kenneth Dover in his recent survey of ancient Greek popular morality notes that the Greek tendency was to think of the individual not as a moral agent but in terms of his usefulness for a function or a purpose. Hence the Greek would ask not, 'How can we be fair to this individual?' but, 'What

[1] *Public and Private Morality*, p. 20.

action . . . is likely to have the best consequences for the strength of the community?'[2]

By contrast, Dover remarks,

> In Western Europe and America a great many people have become accustomed for a very long time to regard the law and the state as mechanisms for the protection of individual freedoms; this attitude has been reinforced by Christian emphasis on the individual's relation to God. We do not take kindly to the notion that there is no religious, moral or domestic claim on the individual which has precedence over the community's claim on his efforts to promote its security and prosperity *vis à vis* other communities.[3]

Historically speaking it can scarcely be denied that Dover is right and that our intense feeling for the value of the individual personality has a Judaeo-Christian origin and simply has not developed to the same extent in other traditions. Nor is this surprising. If every man, no matter what his personal qualities or his social situation, is in a unique relation to God and, in virtue of this relation, has an eternal destiny, it does indeed follow (though it has not always been seen to follow) that he cannot be used merely as a means to political or social ends. The language is reminiscent of Kant and reminds us that Kant himself was aware of the historical connection, and, indeed, emphasized it, while yet denying that this ideal of respect for persons required any theological backing:

> But this is not the only case in which this wonderful religion with its great simplicity of statement has enriched philosophy with far more definite and purer concepts than it had been able to furnish before; but which, once they are there, are freely assented to by Reason and are assumed as concepts to which it could well have come of itself and which it could and should have introduced.[4]

Kant here expresses what one might call the 'matrix theory' of the relation between religion and ethics; that a religious metaphysic provides a matrix within which ethical conceptions develop as a matter of social and cultural history, but of which they are logically independent; so that in due time the matrix can decay leaving the ethic to live its own life. Something like this certainly seems to happen. Indeed it is rather striking how moral ideals tend to achieve their greatest definition and,

[2] *Greek Popular Morality in the Time of Plato and Aristotle,* Blackwell (1974), p. 158.

[3] Op. cit., p. 157.

[4] Kant, *Critique of Judgement,* tr. Bernard, Macmillan (1914), § 91, p. 410 n.

in a sense, their greatest purity, when appeal is no longer made to any metaphysical justification for them. It is as if, the metaphysical crust having been eroded by the winds and rains of critical analysis, the moral strata were laid bare and stood out in lonely eminence. We see this in Kant himself, who is so sure of his *moral* position that he can reverse the traditional order and argue for God's existence as a presupposition of morality. We see it even in Sartre, as Iris Murdoch notices:[5]

> The value of the person is detected by Sartre, not in any patient study of the complexity of human relations, but simply in his experience of the pain of defeat and loss. In cool moments the individual is mercilessly analyzed; his preciousness is apprehended only in the emotional obscurity of a hopeless mourning. ('No human victory can efface this absolute of suffering.') It is as if only one certainty remained; that human beings are irreducibly valuable, without any notion why or how they are valuable or how the value can be defended.

But by the time the process has reached Sartre we have begun to have doubts again. Surely now, not only has the metaphysical crust crumbled entirely, but the morality itself has changed. Sartre no longer means just what Kant meant by the irreducible worth of the human personality (and it may be that even what Kant meant is not quite Christian). How can a man have this sort of worth, if man is what Sartre takes him to be? There is not enough to being a man for the notion to be attached to.

In the Christian tradition to treat another man as having unconditional worth is to show him love in the sense of *agape*. And we have in effect been asking what men would have to be like to be appropriate objects of such love. For it is evident that there are ways of thinking of men which would render it entirely inappropriate. We have, intuitively, a conception of this kind of love, but it is extraordinarily difficult to characterize it without distorting it in one way or another. We want to say that it is because men have, as men, certain qualities and stand in certain relationships, that they are properly to be loved, yet we do not wish such love to be conditional upon the particular characteristics of individuals. Something of what we are inclined to feel about this is expressed with restrained eloquence by McTaggart. In treating of emotions in

[5] *Sartre*, p. 81.

volume ii of *The Nature of Existence* he differentiates between love and all other emotions precisely on this ground:[6]

> My contention is that while love may be because of qualities, it is never in respect of qualities. There are three characteristics of love, as we find it in present experience, which support this view. The first is that love is not necessarily proportional to the dignity or adequacy of the qualities which determine it. A trivial cause may determine the direction of intense love. It may be determined by birth in the same family, or by childhood in the same house. It may be determined by physical beauty, or by purely sexual desire. And yet it may be all that love can be.
>
> Other emotions, no doubt, may be determined by causes not proportioned to them in dignity or adequacy. I may admire a man passionately because he plays football well. I may be proud of myself because of the virtues of my great-grandfather. And so also with acquiescence. I may acquiesce in a state of civil war because it makes the life of a spectator more exciting. But the difference is that, in the case of the other emotions, and the acquiescence, we condemn the result if the cause is trivial and inadequate. The admiration, the pride, and the acquiescence which we have just mentioned would all be condemned because they would be held to be unjustified. But with love, it seems to me, we judge differently. If love does arise, it justifies itself, regardless of what causes produce it. To love one person above all the world for all one's life because her eyes are beautiful when she is young is to be determined to a very great thing by a very small cause. But if what is caused is really love – and this is sometimes the case – it is not condemned on that ground. It is there, and that is enough. This would seem to indicate that the emotion is directed to the person, independently of his qualities, and that the determining qualities are not the justification of that emotion, but only the means by which it arises. If this is so, it is natural that their value should sometimes bear no greater relation to the value of the emotion than the intrinsic value of the key of a safe bears to the value of the gold to which it gives us access.

This is magnificent, and yet it does not quite ring true. As is apparent from the context McTaggart is thinking chiefly of natural human love as experienced in marriage and friendship, and this, we feel, should be more discriminating. We are uncertain in our judgement of Antonio in *The Merchant of Venice* because he is prepared to risk his fortune and his life for so shallow a character as Bassanio. In such a special relationship as that of friendship ought he not to have chosen more wisely and seen more clearly? Yet, even in such a case, if only we were sure that he recognized his friend's shortcomings and stood by him in spite of them, we should regard it as exemplary

[6] *The Nature of Existence*, Vol. ii, Cambridge University Press (1927), p. 152.

love. It would obviously be a mistake to draw too sharp a distinction between the love which depends upon reciprocity and affinity and the love which persists even when these have gone or are temporarily in abeyance. Friendship and marriage as we know them are based upon natural affection reinforced by *agape*—and what McTaggart says does correctly represent what we feel about love in this latter sense, that it does not and ought not to depend on people's distinctive attributes.

That people are not and ought not to be loved in respect of their qualities but for their own sake is not, however, a doctrine that has been universally accepted. Aristotle did not believe it; he thought that people ought to be loved on account of their virtue, and in so far as the good man loves his neighbour as himself, it is only to the extent that he and his neighbour are equally virtuous. It is, as Freud points out, in some ways an outrageous and unnatural suggestion. Freud quotes: 'Thou shalt love thy neighbour as thyself' and continues,

> We will adopt a naive attitude towards it, as if we were meeting for the first time. Thereupon we find ourselves unable to suppress a feeling of astonishment, as at something unnatural. Why should we do this? What good is it to us? Above all, how can we do such a thing? . . . My love seems to me a valuable thing that I have no right to throw away without reflection . . . If I love someone, he must be worthy of it in some way or other . . . He will be worthy of it if he is so like me in important respects that I can love myself in him. . . . I must love him if he is the son of my friend, since the pain my friend would feel if anything untoward happened to him would by my pain – I should have to share it. But if he is a stranger to me and cannot attract me by any value he has in himself or any significance he may already have acquired in my emotional life, it will be hard for me to love him. I shall even be doing wrong if I do, for my love is valued as a privilege by all those belonging to me. . . . But if I am to love him (with that kind of universal love) simply because he too is a denizen of the earth, like an insect or an earthworm or a grass-snake . . . it would be impossible for me to give him as much as by all the laws of reason I am entitled to retain for myself. What is the point of an injunction promulgated with such solemnity, if reason does not recommend it to us? . . . I imagine now I hear a voice gravely adjuring me: 'Just because thy neighbour is not worthy of thy love, is probably full of enmity toward thee, thou shouldst love him as thyself'. I then perceive the case to be like that of *Credo quia absurdum.*[7]

[7] *Civilization and its Discontents* translated by Joan Rivière, The International Psycho-analytical Library (1930), p. 81.

Here this conception of love which Kant describes as 'freely assented to by reason—and to which it would well have come of itself and which it could and would have introduced' is stigmatized by Freud as wholly irrational. And this is one of the puzzling features of the whole discussion. The Christian ethic of love is dismissed on the one hand by those who regard it as totally platitudinous and in no need of any theological justification; on the other by those who characterize it as irrational and so incapable of any justification.[8]

Freud thinks it obvious that 'if I love someone, he must be worthy of it in some way or other' and that I cannot love him 'simply because he too is a denizen of the earth, like an insect or an earthworm or a grass-snake'. He is, of course, rather perverse in the way he draws the contrast. The Western tradition, which he here repudiates, holds that respect is due to man as man, no matter what the individual's qualities, and man is more than a mere denizen of the earth (though, interestingly enough, this feature in the tradition is itself currently under attack from those who blame it for man's spoliation of the non-human world and who favour what they would regard as a Buddhist rather than a Christian emphasis upon the value of *all* sentient being). If man were merely a denizen of the earth he would not have the unique value which the tradition ascribes to him.

Contrast Freud's conception with that of a Christian writer, Thomas Traherne:

> Suppose a curious and fair woman. Some have seen the beauties of Heaven in such a person. It is a vain thing to say they loved too much. I dare say there are ten thousand beauties in that creature which they have not seen. They loved it not too much but upon false causes. Nor so much upon false ones as upon some little ones. They love a creature for sparkling eyes and curled hair, lily breasts and ruddy cheeks; which they should love moreover for being God's image, Queen of the Universe, beloved by Angels, redeemed by Jesus Christ, an heiress of Heaven, and Temple of the Holy Ghost: a mine and fountain of all virtues, a treasury of graces and a child of God. But these excellencies are unknown. They love her perhaps, but do not love God more: nor men as much: nor Heaven and Earth at all. And so, being defective to other things, perish by a seeming excess to that. We should be all Life and Mettle and Vigour and Love to everything and that would poise us. I dare confidently say that every person in the whole world ought to be beloved as much as

[8] Cf. J. L. Mackie, *Ethics*, pp. 130–1.

this: and she if there be any cause of difference more than she is. But God being beloved infinitely more will be infinitely more our joy, and our heart will be more with Him, so that no man can be in danger by loving others too much, that loveth God as he ought.[9]

Traherne is not speaking as a philosopher making careful distinctions. His is the language of poetry, but the copious profusion of images helps to identify the difference that is made by placing man in a religious frame of reference, and to appreciate how rich this frame of reference is. Traherne sees the woman not only as 'redeemed by Jesus Christ' and 'Child of God', but as 'God's image', 'heiress of heaven and Temple of the Holy Ghost', 'a mine and fountain of all virtues', 'a treasury of graces', and, however we interpret these phrases, they clearly imply that men as men possess qualities and capacities for development and response which make them appropriate objects of a divine love of a different order from that which is bestowed upon the rest of the natural world.

It is not possible, therefore, to regard the love of God as an entirely external relation which could be added to or withdrawn from the human situation, leaving everything else unchanged. In the General Thanksgiving, in *The Book of Common Prayer,* we thank God 'for our creation, preservation, and all the blessings of this life', but above all 'for thine inestimable love in the redemption of the world by our Lord Jesus Christ; for the means of grace, and for the hope of glory'. In all these ways God's love is shown and, if we should love one another because God first loved us, it is because we are what God's love has made us and is making us. If men were not constituted in such a way that they were free agents, capable of choosing between good and evil, responding to or rejecting love, they would not be creatures capable of being uniquely related to God, though they would still be creatures and worthy of concern as such; and, if they are so constituted and if their choices and responses are of supreme importance, they deserve, as Kant believed, to be treated as ends and not as means. We may, like Kant, hold that they are in fact so constituted and we may treat them with respect accordingly; or, like Sartre, we may treat them so and not believe that they are so consti-

[9] *Centuries of Meditations,* Betram Dobell, (1908), Second Century, 68, pp. 126 f.

tuted. In each case the question remains whether we have good reason to hold the beliefs about human nature which entitle men to be treated with respect or whether we can continue indefinitely to treat men with respect in the total absence of such beliefs.

There is, as mention of Kant reminds us, a humanistic counterpart to Christian teaching, based upon the respect that is due to any moral agent. For a moral agent is bound to respect himself as a being capable of making moral choices and, by the same token, to respect other moral agents and treat them as ends in themselves, having a peculiar dignity. From this point of view what is wrong with Sartre is that he does not believe that men are, in this sense, moral agents. Kant's own problem is how to provide a coherent conception of human nature which will give moral agency the significance he wishes to attach to it. He attempted to do this by drawing a sharp distinction between the phenomenal self, the self of the desires and the emotions, which belongs to the world as known by the scientist and is subject to determination by scientific laws, and the noumenal self, self as rational will, which enjoys a transcendent freedom. It is the latter which merits respect. But this solution proposes a totally artificial separation between man's intellectual and his emotional life and is thus radically incoherent. Man as moral agent is effectively cut off from everything else that makes him human. The modern secular libertarian requires some other way of vindicating human freedom and the significance of moral choices in a world ruled by chance and necessity.

This discussion has been somewhat abstract, but it is not difficult to see its bearing upon the principle of the sanctity of life, which Hampshire wants to safeguard against utilitarian pressures. The Christian conception of man's nature and destiny makes a significant difference to the status and interpretation of this principle. Consider, for example, the problem of voluntary euthanasia. A case can be made out against it on broadly utilitarian lines. The sufferer needs to be protected against his own rash or ill-considered impulses and against exploitation by others. Importance must also be attached to the interest that others may have in his survival. Moreover society at large must weigh the consequences of any general recognition that doctors may, in certain circumstances, take life or aid in taking it. But, when allowance has been made for all these things, the individual may, on this view, be justified in ending his own life or in consenting to its being ended, if it no longer seems to him worth living. And arguments of this kind, even if taken to be overriding, do not do justice to the conception of the sanctity of life which influences many opponents of euthanasia, both Christian and humanist. They feel that the value of human life is not to be measured by the satisfactions it affords, and that patient acceptance of suffering, infirmity and dependence is an important part of what makes men human. For the humanist this can be seen as belonging to man's dignity as a rational being (although this consideration is more often made to tell the other way). For the Christian it derives from his status as a creature made in the image of God, who holds his life in trust from God and who is never without occasion to serve him even in unspectacular and apparently unproductive ways. The conclusion follows not from a single argument but from a number of converging ones which affect the whole context in which the decision is to be made. Thus the Christian thinks not only of his dependence upon God as Creator but of his gratitude to him, and also of his partaking, through the Holy Spirit, of the sufferings of Christ. The purely secular appeal to human dignity, though not without weight, has, as we have seen, a slighter and less coherent metaphysical background. It is significant that Kant's treatment of suicide[10] is one of those instances in which, in order to reach the desired conclusion, (that the categorical imperative forbids suicide) he appeals to an immanent teleology for which his critical philosophy provides no warrant. Self-love by its nature, he tells us, serves to maintain life.

Kant makes a similar appeal in endeavouring to show that men have a duty to cultivate their talents.[11] They too are given us for a purpose. In the absence of some such consideration it is hard to see why a man should not, if he chooses, take a non-addictive drug which permanently makes the user more contented with his life and less capable of developing his

[10] *Kant, Fundamental Principles of the Metaphysic of Ethics,* translated by T. K. Abbott, Longmans, Green & Co. (1934), p. 47.

[11] Op. cit., p. 48.

talents. It can, of course, be argued, on general utilitarian grounds, that he has a duty to others not to take it; but this is an argument that could on occasion be rebutted. And he may, if he chooses, make self-improvement a Strawsonian personal ideal. But neither approach does justice to the conviction of many conscientious people that it is wrong, and against the individual's interest, to allow his capacity to make responsible decisions to be impaired, even if he wants it to be. Some people might, of course, think otherwise; they might, for example, attach more importance to pleasure and avoidance of pain than to self-determination, and this would reflect fairly fundamental differences in their philosophy of life.

Perhaps one can discern a comparable difference of approach in relation to abortion. Those who regard the foetus as entirely at the disposal of the mother seem to be committed to denying it any share in human status, and this might be because for them experiences are more important than persons. If you attach importance primarily to the person as such you will be impressed by the continuity between the foetus and the person it is to become (if, that is, you do not regard it as a person already). If you attach importance to the person chiefly as the subject of experiences, you will care less about the foetus, which as yet has no experiences and could always be replaced by another potential bearer of experiences. Thus a woman whose ethic is experience-oriented will feel justified in terminating an inconvenient pregnancy and having a child at a more convenient time, whereas one whose ethic is person-oriented will not.

What I am suggesting is that our traditional conception of the sanctity of human life is bound up with our ideas of what it is to be a man and that some of the ideas now current are inadequate to sustain it. As so often Kant is at a turning-point. He has a high estimation of the individual's value, which rests upon his possession, actual or potential, of a good will. But Kant has so dissociated morality from experienced human needs and affections, and the noumenal from the phenomenal self, that we are left wondering in the end just what it is that we are to treat with such respect and why it can exert such categorical claims upon us. What, after all, *is* the Kantian moral agent? He is a rational being who acts in accordance with laws which he is prepared to prescribe universally and who is not at the mercy of 'pathological' desire. Even if it is possible to make sense of this conception, the result would be a somewhat untypical human being. Not only children and imbeciles and, often, the aged are not, in this sense, moral agents, but the greater part of mankind, both today and in the past, have not achieved or even sought this kind of autonomy. Kant's conception of the moral agent and the dignity that attaches to him is both too individualist and too intellectualist to account for the importance we attach to persons. We are reminded of Iris Murdoch's reference to Kant's man and 'the exiguous metaphysical background which Kant was prepared to allow him'. It is not, we feel, the rational being, let alone the potential rational being, but the entire man with all his peculiarities and imperfections, his interests and attachments that it is incumbent upon us to love. As Austin Farrer writes:

> . . . if we sympathize with a man for failing to pursue a good which he does not value in the least, it is difficult to see what we are sympathizing with: not with the man who is, but with some shadow of a man who should be. And realities, not desirabilities, are the objects of regard. I am to love my neighbour, and not my idea of my neighbour . . .[12]

> The regard we owe him is unqualified, because it is owed to God through him. And yet he is no mere channel through which regard is paid to God, for God is regarded by regard to what he regards, and what he regards is the man. The worth of the man is determined by his place in God's purposes; and it is not a worth which in any way hides or palliates his imperfections. For it is measured by the infinite cost at which God is willing to redeem him from them. His worth lies, however, in nothing else than in what he actually is, for this is the subject of divine redemption, this very man whom I know: not, indeed, as God knows him: but in so far as I have any capacity for knowing my fellow-creatures at all, what I know is what God redeems.[13]

It is not difficult to see how a religious frame of reference makes the concept of the sanctity of life intelligible or how some non-religious schemes fail to do so. Nevertheless it may still be objected that the irreducible value of the human person must be entirely independent of any doctrine of man's relationship to God. The objection has been well put by Professor

[12] 'A Moral Argument for the Existence of God' in *Reflective Faith*, S.P.C.K. (1972), p. 123.

[13] Ibid., p. 124.

Downie and Miss Telfer.[14] If it is only in so far as God loves us that we become proper objects of love for each other; if, that is to say, our value as human persons derives from the love which God has for us, 'we are surely not forced to conclude (although some theologians have concluded) that, if we do not presuppose the existence of God, personality thereby loses its value.'

In order to take the measure of this objection we have to make a crucial distinction. Of course, on any showing, 'personality has value,' on the basis of what Mackie calls 'self-referential altruism'.[15] This involves concern for others,

> but for others who have some special connection with oneself; children, parents, friends, workmates, neighbours in the literal, not the metaphorically extended sense. Wider affections than these usually centre upon devotion to some special cause – religious, political, revolutionary, nationalist – not upon the welfare of human beings, let alone sentient beings, in general.

This is the sort of love which alone seemed to Freud to be rational.[16] But it is not this sort of love that is now in question, nor the conception of the value of personality that goes with it. The 'peculiar value, quite beyond the value of any other natural things' which Hampshire seeks to defend is a value which attaches to any human life, no matter how alien that life may be, and demands respect from anyone, no matter who he is or what his relation to the individual whose life is in question. That personality has *this* sort of value is not by any means a truism, as Freud's discussion clearly shows. Freud himself concedes that someone might have value for him if, though not directly related to him, he was the son of his dear friend, and it is by an extension of just this kind that Christians have come to see all men as worthy of regard. For they are all children of one God who loves them equally.

Even this claim, central though it is, is not to be taken as a single compelling argument. The argument itself may take different forms and, in its various forms, is one among a number of interrelated themes. As Gene Outka points out:

> Some . . . rely largely on political imagery. God commands the human agent to love and it is the duty of the agent as servant to obey. In others,

[14] R. S. Downie and Elizabeth Telfer, *Respect for Persons.* Allen & Unwin (1969), p. 36.

[15] *Ethics*, p. 132.

[16] See this chapter, p. 126 above.

familial imagery predominates. It is the will of the heavenly Father that His children obey Him by loving each other. Men should out of gratitude accept their status as children of God and think and act accordingly. Or again: men should love God by conforming to or imitating on their own level and with their own capacities the character of His action. A life of love is consistent with the final purpose of such action, just as non-love frustrates it.[17]

It cannot be God's love for man, taken by itself, that gives man his peculiar value, for God loves all his creatures. But only men, so far as we know, are capable of and destined for eternal life, that is to say, a life of loving communion with God and with other men, which may begin on earth but can be fulfilled only in heaven. This 'cross-reference to eternity', as Herbert Butterfield puts it, makes each man an object of God's protective care as just the individual man that he is, and forbids us to subordinate his fundamental interests to those of the state. Since it is men's capacity to love one another and to love God, rather than their powers of self-legislation, that make men proper objects of respect, and since love involves the entire person, this doctrine escapes the intellectualism which bedevils Kant, but problems still arise as to where the limits of humanity are to be drawn. Here we can only rely on the conviction that what is there to be saved God will save[18] and, where there is doubt, treat with respect all who share the human form.

A further example, in addition to the sanctity of life, is that of fidelity in sexual relationships. The scientific humanist is inclined to argue that there is no need for any specifically sexual morality. Sexual relationships should be governed by the same principles as any others. Care should be taken to see that no unwanted children are born but, so long as that is done, the parties are morally free to decide their own behaviour subject only to the most general moral constraints upon exploitation and injury. Marriage becomes necessary only with the birth of children and is to be thought of primarily as a device for ensuring their maintenance and education. Hence fidelity is not demanded except in so far as it can be shown to affect the stability of the home,[19] unless the parties choose

[17] Gene Outka, *Agape,* Yale University Press (1972), p. 193.

[18] Cf. Austin Farrer, *Love Almighty and Ills Unlimited,* Collins (1962), p. 167.

[19] See Alex Comfort, *Sex in Society,* p. 116, quoted on p. 22 above.

to decide otherwise.

Romantic humanism, by contrast, places considerable emphasis upon the quality of the personal relationship between the partners, and upon the sexual act itself as expressing and confirming their mutual love. This 'personalist' approach results, in one respect, in a comparatively strict moral imperative, for it rules out a sexual relationship from which genuine love is absent. Thus it recognizes a specifically sexual morality; one which, in typically romantic fashion, stresses the spontaneity and authenticity of true erotic love. This makes it impatient of regulation and induces a certain tension between the impulse to permanence, which follows from the seriousness with which the relationship is viewed, and the conviction that it should last only as long as spontaneous love itself lasts and no longer. Hence fidelity has a value which is more than merely instrumental, but is nevertheless not unconditional.

In practice the modern secular mind seeks an accommodation between these two positions. Society requires some regulation of sexual relationships, especially where the interests of children are concerned. Although a variety of patterns of the institution of marriage might suffice for this essential function, monogamy is favoured because there are good utilitarian arguments for it, and also because it is a better vehicle for romantic love than the available alternatives. But the result is a somewhat uneasy compromise. The romantic tends to regard the restraints imposed upon him by society as an artificial restriction upon what ought ideally to be a free and unfettered relationship. And the sort and degree of fidelity between the partners which is consistent with the romantic ideal is not in any way directed to, or particularly apt for, the secure upbringing of children, which is what the rationalist is chiefly interested in.

What is missing in both these views, and therefore in the attempted accommodation between them, is the conception of fidelity as an unconditional demand, which belongs intrinsically to marriage and is neither the result simply of utilitarian contrivance nor subject to the changing attitudes of those involved; the conception to which the marriage vows in the Prayer Book service give such memorable and moving expression: 'to have and to hold from this day forward, for better or for worse, for richer for poorer, in sickness and in health, to love and to cherish, till death us do part.' Although 'according to God's holy ordinance' this is not a matter simply of divine command. It answers the needs of the human heart for assurance of continuing love and care and for the opportunity to grow together in complete confidence and trust. There is, as Mr J. R. Lucas puts it, an 'inner logic' in favour of permanence, since without it love must be kept partly in reserve.[20] And permanence cannot be made to depend on the continuance and continuity of romantic love alone; *eros* requires to be reinforced by *agape*. It follows that the secure love which children need does not, on this view, run counter to the 'logic' of the relationship between the parents, but flows naturally from it.

Fidelity, so understood, is an important element in the Western ethical tradition and one which is honoured and exemplified in the lives of many who are not professing Christians. They can recognize its 'inner logic' and verify it in their own experience. But it has come under increasing pressure from conceptions of human nature which are difficult, if not impossible, to reconcile with it. Essential to it is a conviction that the institution of marriage has an appropriateness which is not the product simply of individual or social choice; that, in some sense of the word, it is natural rather than merely conventional. This conviction makes itself felt even in the purely romantic view of sex, for its central contention is that the sexual act is the uniquely appropriate expression of profound erotic love and *therefore* not to be engaged in in its absence. It is not simply that it can be given this significance, if the partners choose (for plainly it can also be made to express very different emotions), but that this is, in some sense, its true significance. It is as if it had a quasi-sacramental character. But in a modern secular world-view there is no room for such notions (though there was, perhaps, to some extent in paganism).

I have given some examples of the way in which, and the reasons for which, certain moral principles are given more

[20] J. R. Lucas, in an appendix to *Marriage and the Church's Task*, Report of the General Synod Marriage Commission, Church Information Office (1978), p. 125.

weight in a Christian scheme of thought than they merit on broadly utilitarian grounds. I have not attempted to discuss the enormously difficult question whether any of them are entirely exceptionless.[21] I am content to accept Hampshire's formulation when he speaks of moral prohibitions which are 'more or less insurmountable, except in abnormal, painful and improbable circumstances'. It is sufficient for the purposes of my argument to claim that such principles, to which the man of traditional conscience is characteristically committed, are more congruous with a religious view of the world than with a modern secular one.

[21] For a thorough discussion see Donald Evans, 'Paul Ramsey on Exceptionless Moral Rules' in *Love and Society,* edd. James Johnson and David Smith, American Academy of Religion and Scholars Press (1974), and the writings of Paul Ramsey to which he refers.

10

Religion, Scepticism, and the Demands of Autonomy

It has been argued in the last chapter that theism can provide a justification for demands upon the conscience that are categorical and virtually absolute, that can be overridden, as Hampshire puts it, only in 'abnormal, painful and improbable circumstances'. The chief example used was Hampshire's own, the principle of the sanctity of human life. No principle strong enough to satisfy the traditional conscience can be yielded by utilitarian reasoning, and no form of subjectivism can give the demand the categorical character which it has for the traditional conscience.

But the further question may now be pressed: why should the individual acknowledge the authority of morality at all? A straightforward and, at first sight, uncontroversial answer can be offered along the lines of my earlier excursus into moral philosophy. In outline it would run as follows. Human life is such that people have needs which can be met and purposes which can be realized only if they recognize obligations to help one another and to refrain from harming one another in certain specifiable ways. Some of these needs are basic, belonging to all men everywhere; some are defined in terms of institutions which are not thus universal, but which represent alternative ways of satisfying basic human needs. Thus morality is not arbitrary, but is rooted in the social nature of man. It is in this context that moral reasoning finds its place. Since no man can attain maturity and become capable of making choices and forming purposes except in a society of some kind there is a palpable irrationality, amounting to a sort of pragmatic contradiction, in a man's rejecting morality altogether.

Let us suppose that the immoralist recognizes that there is such an institution as morality and that we have adequately explained its rationale, yet declines to be impressed. He does not see why he personally should embrace a system which requires him to put himself out for the sake of other people. Have we any means of convincing him? We might point out[1] that, if he refuses to acknowledge moral reasons for acting in ways that will help others, he cannot invoke moral arguments for other people acting in ways that will help him. To this he may reply that he can perfectly well invoke such arguments if he wishes; we have only shown that he is not morally entitled to invoke them, which he does not deny. Since people are often moved by them he has the best possible grounds of prudence for employing them. We may then have recourse to prudential arguments ourselves. We may argue that, since society depends on mutual acceptance of obligations, a man who enjoys the advantages of society, while repudiating its obligations, is cheating his neighbours and is in grave danger of being found out and cut off from society:[2] and, furthermore, that, even if he succeeds in evading detection, this policy of concealment must restrict that 'free and unfeigned intercourse with our fellows', which is an essential condition of human happiness.[3] This argument, he may concede, has some force, but it has most force against the individual who proposes to act on the principle of never doing what the conscientious man would do. It would count comparatively little against the man who simply limits his moral liabilities to his immediate circle and, within that, to those situations which do not make inordinate demands upon him. And, as Plato saw, it would be powerless against the holder of the ring of Gyges who could be sure of appearing moral, while freely practising immorality.

The problem has been perceptively discussed by Mr G. J. Warnock in his book, *The Object of Morality*.[4] He takes a view of morality very close to mine and then asks two questions, whether a reasonable man *must* acknowledge the force of moral reasons and whether a reasonable man must regard moral reasons as overriding. He answers both questions in the negative. In respect of the first he argues that the institution of morality, as he has described it, presupposes that it is a

[1] Cf. Hare, *Freedom and Reason*, p. 101.

[2] Cf. Hobbes, *Leviathan*, Bk I, chapter 15.

[3] Cf. Hume, *Enquiry Concerning the Principles of Morals*, ed. Selby-Bigge, O.U.P. (1966), p. 283.

[4] Methuen (1971).

good thing to avoid the deprivations and sufferings which would result from its abandonment, for

> if no help is forthcoming, success goes to those strong enough, resourceful enough, to succeed without help; 'injustice' denies goods to those with no 'natural' claim to them. Why, it may be asked, should the weak and undistinguished, the helpless and dependent, be protected from the natural consequences of their contemptible condition? Why should the formidable and strong, the self-sufficient and intelligent, be denied the fruits of their natural advantages? . . . It is as if, in morality, there were incorporated a kind of question-begging egalitarian democracy; we have mentioned already the idea of 'respect for persons' but what is there, after all, in most persons that merits respect? Or what in their 'nature' confers any rights upon them?[5]

Warnock here somewhat understimates the damage that would be done by the universal abandonment of morality. For, as Hobbes recognizes, even the strong and resourceful would find life 'nasty, brutish and short' in the absence of the mutual assistance that only some kind of morality can provide. All the same, the sort and degree of morality needed to enable the strong effectively to exploit their strength could be pretty minimal; and in any case the immoralist is frankly prepared to be parasitic upon a society which is kept going to his advantage by the morality of other men.

In respect of the second question—whether a reasonable man must regard moral reasons as overriding—he suggests that someone who does not go as far as the extreme immoralist and reject morality entirely might nevertheless think other things sometimes more important than morality.

> If I believe that I am capable of composing, say, magnificent music, is it irrational to think that I should, if necessary, neglect my obligations to my dependent wife, children, and aged parents in order to do so? I might, of course, in such cases believe myself *morally* justified; I might hold that my . . . music . . . constituted a contribution to the well-being of persons, possibly of posterity, which *morally* outweighed the moral claims of those more immediately detrimentally affected. But I think I need not do so. It seems to me possible to see in, say, aesthetic objects a value for themselves, not merely for their place in the lives of people in general, which, if so, may sometimes be weighed *against* moral values, and by some may sometimes be regarded as of greater weight.[6]

So he sums up the question: 'What if I value beauty, say, more highly than justice? "Creativity", or some such thing, more

[5] *Object of Morality*, p. 160.

[6] Op. cit., p. 158.

highly than moral conscientiousness? I do not see that reason rules decisively against such valuations.'[7] Warnock's discussion is interesting in the way it parallels the train of thought by which, as I argued earlier, romantic humanism characteristically departed from the old enlightenment certainties, first elevating creativity above conscientiousness and then calling conscience itself entirely in question. We might pose Warnock's question as being how to deal with the romantic who takes this line. At this point he suggests, tantalizingly, that 'we might do the trick with the aid of a deity' but does not develop this suggestion. Instead he concludes that 'the recognition of "the moral law" as an *efficacious* and predominant determinant of practical judgement and action cannot be forced, so to speak, *a priori* upon rational beings.'

He is then left with the question how it is that people do after all, for the most part, accept the moral point of view. 'If, as rational beings, they do not *have* to do so, how is it that they do?' And he answers, somewhat lamely, 'the brief answer here has to be, I think, simply that it is possible for them to come to *want* to. . . . One can want to acquire and exercise the settled disposition to comply with such principles in one's judgement and conduct, to give due weight to the range of reasons that those principles generate.'[8] It is interesting to notice that, when pressed, Hare comes up with essentially the same answer. Normally he does not raise the question *why* we should regulate our lives by universal prescriptive principles and *why* such principles should be overriding. He is inclined to echo Prichard's criticism of Plato and to claim that no satisfactory answer to this question is conceivable. For either the reason produced will be a prudential one (the just man will be happy) or it will be a moral one. But the man who does his duty as a means to happiness is not acting from a moral motive, so what is justified in this way is not really morality; and to appeal to moral reasons is circular. And there is no third 'ought' in terms of which to adjudicate between the moral and the non-moral life. A man simply has to decide, and will generally decide in accordance with his education. Hence for Hare, as for Aristotle, it is essential that children should be 'well brought up', so that they want to do what is right.

[7] Op. cit., p. 159.

[8] Op. cit., p. 165.

This is true so far as it goes, but in our present cultural situation it only takes the problem one stage further back. Educationalists cannot make up their minds what they ought to be doing. Should they be handing on a traditional morality; or encouraging the child to be critical and creative; or tempering this latter policy with insistence upon some basic social rules; or just trying to promote the child's psychological health? Even if agreement could be reached about a basic morality, some would doubt whether society ought to do more than develop in the young the capacity to reason for themselves about moral questions, even if the result of their reasoning were to be the rejection of morality altogether, as presumably it might be. Our present situation, in fact, closely resembles the one that Plato encountered when the loss of confidence in a traditional ethic made it a problem how to teach virtue and compelled him to raise fundamental problems about the justification of morality before tackling the task of moral education.

Nevertheless, as Prichard's critique of Plato shows, it is extremely difficult to deal with this question without declining into insensitivity or simple falsehood. The danger can be seen most clearly in Cicero because of his greater crudity. He faces the question in the *De officiis* and dissolves the problem by maintaining stoutly that whatever is morally good is expedient, and, whatever is expedient is morally good. But in attempting to establish this he oscillates continually between claiming that the good man will always have an enjoyable life in a thoroughly down to earth sense, and arguing high-mindedly that he will be rewarded in the only way appropriate to a rational being, viz. by being enabled to exhibit moral virtue; i.e., between 'honesty pays' and 'virtue is its own reward'. The down to earth claim is plainly untrue and is not high-minded enough. Morality is more than prudence. But the high-minded contention that 'virtue is its own reward' is doubly unsatisfying. If moral virtue is what we have all along supposed it to be, a principled concern for others' needs, then those needs matter or virtue so conceived is pointless. And if other men's happiness, at which the good man ought to aim, is distinct from their virtue, the good man's own happiness cannot consist in his virtue alone. Hence for all its high-minded nobility Iris Murdoch's declaration cannot stand: 'The humble man . . . sees the pointlessness of virtue and its unique value and the endless extent of its demand.' Self-sacrifice is not pointless; it intends that other people may live and flourish. It is the supreme test of love and even the supreme expression of love, but it is not the supreme fruition of love. There is need, as Kant saw, for some connection between virtue and happiness of a down to earth kind. Something can be done to bring the two positions together, the down-to-earth and the high-minded, by insisting with Plato and Aristotle on the contentment which attends the life of moral virtue, which is the highest and purest pleasure and flows from the recognition that one is achieving excellence as a man. But Aristotle, at least, saw that there is more to happiness than this; it may be an essential element in human flourishing, but it is not the fullness of it. And it becomes apparent from the words of Christ: 'If ye, then, being evil, know how to give good gifts unto your children, how much more shall your father which is in heaven give good things to them that ask him.' No human father, if it was in his power to give his children more, would be satisfied with giving them only the opportunity to be virtuous and the contentment that flows from it. He would want them to enjoy all the happiness that life can afford.

Warnock remarks that 'one could do the trick with the aid of a deity'. How? For the trick to be done God's purpose for men would have to be such that it cannot be achieved without the pursuit of moral virtue, but not such that it consists simply in the achievement of moral virtue. He who would save his soul must be willing to lose it, but there must be more to saving one's soul than just the willingness to lose it. And this is indeed Christian teaching. No one can enter into the Kingdom of Heaven who has not ceased to make himself the centre of his world, but the blessedness he then enjoys is at the same time the fulfilment of his own deepest longings. We have an image of this in marriage. The love which alone makes possible the fullest mutual enjoyment and fruition is the love which holds in sickness or in health, for better or for worse; but the presence of this love does not exhaust the riches of the marriage. So when Iris Murdoch writes: 'The acceptance of death is an acceptance of our own nothingness which is an automatic spur to our concern with what is not ourselves,'[9] we are aware of some slight, but significant distortion of the Christian ethic. The love of others, which the Christian ethic demands, involves an active concern for their well-being, and that in turn implies a clear conception of what is best for them, which must, in consistency, be also in essentials what is best for ourselves. It is not that we accept our own nothingness and this automatically brings concern with what is not ourselves (as a Stoic or a Buddhist might hold), but rather that in so far as we lose ourselves in the love and worship of God we are able to show a true regard both for others and for ourselves. The reluctance of the high-minded to accept this is associated with their suspicion that it reduces morality in the end, despite protestations to the contrary, to a sort of self-interested prudence. When the hymn writer declares:

My God I love thee not because
I hope for heaven thereby,
Nor yet because who love thee not
Are lost eternally,

they feel that any clear recognition of the considerations mentioned in this verse must have the effect of corrupting motives. And this is perhaps what Iris Murdoch has in mind when she writes that 'almost everything that consoles us is a fake . . . In the case of the idea of a transcendent personal God the degeneration of the idea seems scarcely avoidable.'[10] The possibility of such corruption cannot be denied and it is matched by a comparable temptation to the high-minded from the thought that he is superior to others in the purity of his devotion to duty for its own sake; it is hard for this ideal not to degenerate into pharisaism. But if a man longs for a heaven that is a genuine communion with God and with other men, what he hopes for is not self-interested in any objectionable sense, for he desires this for others as well as for himself; and, if he does not, then he has not yet made the required *metanoia*—he has not repented. He has to be born again, but what he then receives is what he most deeply wants, a bliss that cannot be enjoyed without selfless devotion to God and to others.

When understood in this way—a profoundly traditional

[9] *The Sovereignty of Good*, p. 59.

[10] Ibid.

way—the emphasis in the Gospels upon heaven and hell can be seen to fulfil morality, not to distort it. Richard Robinson writes in his *An Atheist's Values*:

> . . . the reasons that Jesus gave for his precepts, namely his promises and threats, are quite unacceptable. They are false, since there is no heaven or hell; and anyhow they make his precepts precepts of prudence instead of precepts of morality. To obey rules because otherwise you will go to hell is prudence, not morality. The good and moral reason for a moral precept is that its reign in a society lessens misery in that society.[11]

Robinson's protest is understandable but misplaced. Although 'good and moral reasons' are more various than he suggests, it is only in so far as a man is genuinely moved by them that he is able to enter and enjoy the blessedness of heaven, and only in so far as he consistently rejects them that he 'loses his soul'—and discovers with Sartre that 'hell is other people'.

So one way in which the Christian can reply to the immoralist is to claim that it is an essential part of God's purpose for man that he can fulfil his nature and achieve what will ultimately content him only if he ceases to make himself the centre of his own universe; hence the demands of morality—of principled concern for the needs of others—are both objective and categorical. This is not, of course, the whole answer. There are other strands in the Christian understanding of morality which reinforce the one I have chosen to develop. It is, above all, the love of God which serves both as a motive and as a reason for the love of neighbour. We should love him because he first loved us; and we should love others because he loves them. It is this theme preeminently which explains how it is *possible* for a man to turn away from anxious self-concern and identify himself with the interests of others, however uncongenial those others are, and even if it runs counter to the prevailing ethos of his society.

But Robinson's protest suggests a further and even more fundamental objection to the entire argument of this book. I have claimed that some of the dominant themes of the ethical tradition of the West are bound up with Christianity not only as a matter of history, but also as a matter of logic—that is to say that religious premisses are required for an adequate rationale of them. And I have made this part of

[11] Oxford University Press (1964), p. 155.

a more general contention that, once the limits of a platitudinous morality are passed, moral systems and moral theories, both secular and religious, reflect a 'vision of life'. In this way I have argued the need for a metaphysic of ethics. In exploring the dilemmas of the traditional conscience I have insisted that moral intuitions cannot be accepted as entirely self-authenticating but require to be given a rationale in terms of a total view of life. And I have claimed that Plato and Aristotle are to be preferred to most post-Kantian moral philosophers precisely for the reason that, although they rely upon ethical intuition, they see the need to justify their doing so. The objection I have in mind is directed against the logical possibility of any such justification.

The objection is one that is often given a cursory treatment in the opening chapter of introductory books on moral philosophy and is then taken as absolving the writers from any obligation to explore further the relation between religion and morality. I have, instead, left it till the last, because such force as the argument of this book possesses itself creates a presumption against the validity of this objection. The argument is to the effect that Christianity, or any religion, or, for that matter, any world-view can have ethical implications only if acceptance of it in the first place commits the believer to certain ethical principles. For this reason these principles are logically primary and the system as a whole cannot serve to justify them. Any proposed justification would be viciously circular. We need independent moral judgement to interpret and assess any system of religious belief which makes ethical claims.

Though presented in various forms, the essential feature of the argument is that it confronts the advocate of a religious ethic with a dilemma: *either* we ought to do what is right because it is right (this being why God has commanded it), *or* we ought to do the action just because God has commanded it. If the first alternative is accepted, what fundamentally determines our moral choice is not our religious belief, but the moral judgment, which we make independently, that the action is right. If the second, then God's command becomes a mere arbitrary fiat with no ethical significance. The most monstrous cruelty would become right if God were to command it. Either way, religion has no bearing on morals; morality is entirely independent of religion.[12] There are two initial points to notice about this argument. The first is that it is designed to refute a single extreme position about the relation between religion and morality, viz. that morality is wholly derivative from and dependent upon religious belief, indeed that the moral 'ought' can be *defined* in terms of God's commands. This having been taken as refuted, it is then assumed that the argument has also demonstrated the impossibility of religious belief having any logical bearing upon the status, scope or content of morality. But it is one thing to hold that religious belief may profoundly affect a man's beliefs as to how he should live, and why he should live in that way, and another to claim that morality must be wholly based upon considerations which are specifically religious. The second point is that the argument is generally expressed, as here, in terms of the assumption that a religious morality will be exclusively a morality of divine commands. It is true that language of this sort has a part to play in the Judaeo-Christian tradition, but religious morality may also be conceived in terms of copying a pattern or example—the imitation of Christ. The failure to notice this not only betrays a certain insensitivity on the part of the critics to the range and complexity of Christian ethics, but as will appear later, invites positive errors of interpretation.

However, this does not affect the logical point, which can be put equally well in terms of a religious pattern-morality as in terms of a religious law-morality. For suppose we say that Christian morality consists in the imitation of Christ. The critic can always ask: 'Why choose *this* exemplar?' and the only satisfactory answer from a moral point of view, it will be said, is 'Because He is a good pattern to follow.' 'But', the critic continues, 'To recognize a pattern as a good one is to possess criteria which could be specified in an ethical major premiss of the form "A man is a good man to imitate if and only if he displays characteristics x, y and z.".' For a man who possesses these criteria the pattern may of course be of practical use, for, as Dr Johnson remarked: 'example is always more efficacious than precept'; but from a theoretical point

[12] A version of the argument first appears in Plato's *Euthyphro*, 10 a–d.

of view it cannot tell him more than he already knows. A man who lacks these criteria will have no good reason for choosing this pattern in preference to any other. The point is made concisely in the familiar remark of Kant's in the *Grundlegung*: 'Even the Holy One of the Gospels must first be compared with our ideal of moral perfection, before we can recognise him as such.'[13]

It is important to notice that the argument is perfectly general and applies as much to Aristotle and his *phronimos* as to the Christian and Christ. Aristotle's advice is to copy the *phronimos*, the man of practical wisdom; but this presupposes that one can recognise a *phronimos* when one sees him; but this in turn presupposes that one already knows the sort of thing the *phronimos* does and says; but, if one knows that, there is no need to copy the *phronimos*. As Hare puts it, 'We have first to satisfy ourselves that a man is good before we can be sure that he is *phronimos* . . . i.e. we should have to make for ourselves the sort of moral judgements we thought we were going to get made for us by the *phronimos*.'[14]

Now this has the air of a simple and conclusive argument, which is what philosophers have generally taken it to be. It is, however, highly paradoxical, for it appears to prove the logical impossibility of a process with which we are all perfectly familiar—the process by which we develop spiritually (and in every other way) by taking people we admire for models and imitating them. We do seek the advice of wise men, as we should scarcely do if we knew in advance what advice they would give. This process requires that one possess some incipient awareness of what is worth imitating; it evidently does not require that one possess a full understanding of the virtues which the model possesses and which one hopes to acquire by imitating him. It does not, fortunately, take a saint to recognize a saint, a genius to recognize a genius, the master of a trade to recognize a master, a *phronimos* to recognize a *phronimos*. If you want to become a good rugby player, it is a sound plan to choose an outstanding player and model yourself on him. Of course, in order to recognize that he *is*

[13] *Fundamental Principles of the Metaphysics of Ethics*, p. 30.

[14] In a personal communication; cf. *Applications of Moral Philosophy*, Macmillan (1972), p. 5.

a good player you must have some rudimentary knowledge of the game. If you went to the Varsity match, without even this rudimentary knowledge, you might be forgiven for forming the idea that it was a contest of brute physical strength and that the big man who was delivering uppercuts out of sight of the referee was the man to model yourself on. But a little elementary instruction in the basic laws of the game would be enough to set you looking for the appropriate qualities. You can then choose a model and learn the game by following him. Similarly in the moral case. 'Live like x' is useless advice unless you have some idea in what respect you are to copy x. You must have some notion of human virtue. But here too we can recognize what is excellent without being able to determine it entirely for ourselves from scratch. In these circumstances when we choose someone for our model not only do we not in fact already know the major premiss 'the man to copy is the man who displays such and such precise characteristics; or who behaves in such and such a determinate way in such and such a situation'; it is not clear that we ever can state precisely what these characteristics are, however much we ourselves may advance in our understanding of the relevant virtues. It may be that this is a sort of knowledge which not only the tyro, but also the expert is without because it is logically impossible to have it. If this is so, as I think it is (though I shall not try to argue it now) a given pattern–morality is not logically translatable into a set of rules or principles or commands. 'Act like the *phronimos*' cannot be rendered by 'Do x, y . . . z in such and such circumstances', and it was because Aristotle recognized this that he attached such importance to the good man as the canon and measure of virtue. Thus we do, as Hare recognizes, respect the judgement of the wise man and what we look for is, as a rule, not just some plain instructions as to what to do, but the setting of our problem in a wider context and a deeper understanding of the issues involved. It is a psychological commonplace that we often extend our horizons in just this way, and could scarcely develop otherwise. The dilemma, as originally proposed, gains its apparent force by posing false alternatives, viz. *either* you have already full understanding of the virtues the model exemplifies, *or* you know nothing and therefore cannot choose your model.

The dilemma is the same, and so is the solution, in the case of law-morality. Just as, in the case of pattern morality, it does not require the same degree of moral insight to choose a model or exemplar as the latter himself possesses; so, in the case of law-morality, it does not require the same degree of moral insight to determine that a lawgiver is worthy of obedience as it does for the lawgiver to determine the laws. It is entirely possible that Moses should recognize God (in Nowell-Smith's quaint phrase) as 'a morally competent authority' without being able himself to invent or discover the commandments given to him on Mt. Sinai. No doubt this suggestion, as it stands, strikes one as absurd, but the absurdity is not logical; it derives from the theological *naïveté* of the terms in which the problem is being discussed. It is only in the context of coherent theological doctrine that we can expect to understand how men can come to recognize the goodness of God. It is true that, if we are to say, for whatever reasons, that God is good, we must give 'good' some meaning not expressly derived from 'God'; but it does not follow that the only sufficient reason for believing God to be good is our own ability, independently, to think up the divine decrees for ourselves.

Why do the critics insist upon this paradoxical contention? The reason is, I think, that they believe themselves to be committed to it by a fundamental principle which must at all costs be maintained. This is the principle of autonomy. At any stage you like to take in this process of moral and spiritual development, they want to say, when the religious man decides to obey this law of God, or to imitate Christ in this respect, he either makes a moral decision or he does not. Only if he does make a moral decision does his action have moral significance (this is a tautology). Otherwise the obedience or the imitation, as the case may be, flows from some motive of fear or prudence or affection and there is nothing moral about it. It is, in Kant's terminology 'heteronomous'. The point is made by Nowell-Smith:

Unless we accept Hobbes' consistent but repugnant equation of God's right with his might, we must be persuaded independently of His goodness before we admit His right to command. We must judge for ourselves whether the Bible is the inspired word of a just and benevolent God or a curious amalgam of profound wisdom and gross superstition. To judge this is to make a moral decision, so that in the end far from morality being based on religion, religion is based on morality.[15]

There is, however, I suggest, an ambiguity in the notion of the autonomy of ethics in this connection. To assert the autonomy of morals may be to assert the independence of ethics from religion either in the sense that morality must have the *sole* word or in the sense that it is to have a *decisive* word. What I mean is this: it is one thing to say that if a practice (such as human sacrifice) is immoral, the religion that enjoins or permits it is discredited; and another to say that religion can have no part in determining whether a practice is immoral.

It is possible to maintain the autonomy of morals by insisting that the matter is settled once the moral point has been proved, and cannot be settled until it has been proved, whilst still allowing that religious considerations may be relevant to the decision on the moral point. For instance, if you believe that morality is in some way based upon the fundamental needs of men, you may concede to religion some say as to what the fundamental needs of men are. The distinction may be put differently (if very crudely) thus: someone who maintains the autonomy of ethics may be thinking of religion and morality as two distinct and entirely independent subjects, such that, once the question at issue has been identified as moral, we know without further ado that no religious considerations come into it. Or he may conceive of moral thinking as a discipline which can and must take account of any considerations, including religious ones, which can be shown to be morally relevant. The distinction (though crudely put) is vital to this discussion. The autonomy of morals, on the former interpretation, rules out any logical bearing of religion upon morals *ex hypothesi*; on the latter interpretation it remains an open question whether and to what extent religious evidence is admissible in a court of morals. In other words the assumption that is generally made in framing the argument from autonomy is that we already have available a complete and fully specified moral system and that by reference to this we can and should test any religious or metaphysical claims. The

[15] P. H. Nowell-Smith, 'Morality: Religious and Secular' in *The Rationalist Annual 1961*.

latter cannot, therefore, contribute to our understanding of morality. This is an assumption that comes easily to Kantians or intuitionists. But if, instead, we place morality in the context of human needs and insist that moral judgements require to be supported by reasons, and that these reasons must relate to some intelligible and defensible conception of human well-being, it becomes clear that an adequate understanding of morality is no longer attainable in total independence of our beliefs about the nature and destiny of man. There are, no doubt, as we saw in our discussion of 'moral platitudes', some moral virtues, such as courage, honesty and justice which are such obvious conditions of well-being that any moral system must recognize them, but once we get beyond them (and even they need specifying), what we are committed to is a process of moral reasoning rather than a determinate set of moral principles (which is not to say that the reasoning does not yield principles). A capacity for moral reasoning and for moral development is something that men must be presumed to have in virtue of being men and represents the only sort of autonomy that they require. Their possession of this capacity is not the least of those things that an adequate conception of human nature must account for.

Whatever the truth may be, it is clear, I think, that the type of argument I have been considering does not prove the autonomy of morals in the narrower sense (that morality must have the *sole* word) but only in the wider sense (that morality must have *a decisive* word); and that is so wide as to give most advocates of a religious ethic all the room they want. What the argument shows is that, in order to influence morality, religion must, so to speak, argue her case and argue it in moral terms—that is, in terms which an active intelligence and a sensitive conscience can be persuaded to recognize as morally significant. But this does *not* entail that they must be terms which were already clearly grasped and understood before the dialogue with religion got under way. This is why Kant's famous remark is so preposterous: 'Even the Holy One of the Gospels must first be compared with our ideal of moral perfection before we can recognise him as such.' It is absurd to suppose that the fisherman of Galilee—when he made the confession: 'Thou art Christ, the Son of the Living God'—had compared

Jesus with his ideal of moral perfection (just as it was before any encounter took place) and had satisfied himself that he had, so to speak, achieved the required standard. He had, of course, judged for himself, and in judging he exercised moral insight, but he could not himself have preached the Sermon on the Mount.

It is, indeed, often misleading to talk, as I did earlier, about choosing a model for imitation; what more often happens is that the model, by its sheer impressiveness, demands our imitation and in so doing not merely develops, but radically revises, our previous notions about what is worth imitating. If such acceptance is not to be uncritical fanaticism it must be possible for us to justify it, although it is evidently not necessary, or possible, for us to justify it wholly in terms that were available to us before we encountered the new paradigm. There is an analogy here with the process by which, as Eliot maintains, a great artist creates the standards by which he is to be judged. Autonomy requires that the standards used shall be, in some sense, the judge's own standards; not, however, in the sense that he must have invented them; only in the sense that he must have rationally accepted them. The logical force of Kant's dictum is simply that recognition of Christ's moral perfection is in itself a moral act, and this we cannot and need not deny.

It may, however, be objected that, in developing this argument, I have in fact gone no further than the 'matrix theory' which at an earlier stage I attributed to Kant.[16] Christianity has introduced 'more definite and purer concepts than [philosophy] had been able to furnish before; but which, once they are there, are truly assented to by reason and are assumed as concepts to which it could well have come of itself and which it could and would have introduced.' For we could in principle have thought out the moves which the great athlete discloses to us or the advice which we receive from the *phronimos*. And similarly we could in principle arrive unaided at whatever moral insights we derived from revealed religion.

In order to take the measure of this objection we must, I think, ask what is the force of 'could in principle'. It might mean, I suggest:

[16] Above, p. 123.

(i) 'It is logically possible that we should have arrived at these insights.' This is undeniable but uninteresting.
(ii) 'We had the capacity to arrive at these insights' or at least '*some* men had this capacity.'
(iii) 'These insights were derivable from, or implicit in, moral beliefs already held.'

It seems to me quite clear that original ideas in any field need not be derivable, and generally are not derivable, from ideas already held; also that those who come to accept them need not, although they may, be able to hit upon them themselves. Hence in relation to genuine originality of any kind whether in morality, science or the arts:

(a) It is not necessary, in order to recognize the answer to a problem, that one should already independently have discovered that answer;
(b) It is not necessary that one could have derived the answer from already accepted beliefs;
(c) It is not necessary, though it may be the case, that one could, unaided, have hit upon the answer;
(d) It *is* necessary that one should be able to understand how it does provide the answer to the problem, and this demands a suitable background of knowledge and an adequate understanding of the state of the question up to that point.

The critic, therefore, has not succeeded in showing that religion could not introduce genuinely original moral insights or that, if it did, the moral autonomy of those who received and recognized them *as* moral insights would be in one way impugned. Nevertheless, so far as this argument goes, there is no reason for supposing that religion was needed to achieve these insights. The position is the same as with Aristotle's *phronimos*; we could, with no loss of moral autonomy, in fact owe new moral insights to him, but we might ourselves have hit upon them quite independently of him. We might indeed; but we must recognize what this would entail. In order to do so we should ourselves have needed to be able to place our problem in the wider context in which the *phronimos* viewed it. For it was his appreciation of this which enabled him to advise us. Similarly, as I have been arguing, for a fuller understanding, indeed, an adequate justification, of morality a theistic metaphysic is required. In the light of this we can see that men are so made that they can fulfil their natures and achieve lasting satisfaction ('solid joys and lasting pleasures') only if they follow a certain way of life, respecting the principles and developing the virtues which are needed to express and maintain that way of life.[17] If this is true, Kant's dictum remains correct but does not, as he thought, make the influence of religion superfluous. For 'philosophy could and would have introduced' the 'more definite and purer concepts' to which he refers only if it was a philosophy in which these concepts were at home. And a theistic philosophy might alone satisfy this requirement.

But a stronger objection than this might be intended. So far as the argument goes up to this point, it could be said, the difference that religion makes to morality remains almost entirely an external one. It provides a warrant, otherwise lacking, for viewing morality as objective; it allows the concept of human nature to have some content other than what we choose to give it; it makes it reasonable for us to take our moral intuitions seriously (though not to rely upon them uncritically); it deepens our understanding of human needs, and gives the moral 'ought' the force of a categorical demand. God, however, appears for the most part—or so an unsympathetic critic might allege—rather like Prospero, or the Duke in *Measure for Measure*, as a benevolent paternalist who, having created the world, and granted men an eternal destiny, remains himself to them creator and lawgiver, but no more. This is the impression created, for example, by Mackie's extremely fair and sympathetic attempt to demonstrate the logical coherence of a theistic ethic: 'The picture of God as an arbitrary tyrant is replaced by the belief that he demands of his creatures only that they should live in what will be, for them, the most satisfying way.'[18] This is, so far as it goes, true but it leaves out one essential feature of the Christian view of ethics. God enters into it not simply as a guarantee of the seriousness of the moral demand or of its objectivity and meaning, but as

[17] Cf. Mackie, *Ethics*, p. 239.

[18] Mackie, op. cit., p. 231. Mackie believes that such a theological ethic is coherent, but that belief in God is not coherent.

himself the goal of the entire human pilgrimage. So, as Helen Oppenheimer puts it:

> God in his wisdom made the human race in such-and-such a way (here a Christian anthropology would have to be spelled out); and in finding and realizing the true pattern of our natures, complex and mysterious as it is and only distinguishable with patience, we are, in the same process, glorifying God and entering the kingdom of heaven.[19]

So the enjoyment of God and of his creatures through him is not simply something added as an extra to the concerns of our present life, but our present life, with all its moral demands, is an instalment and anticipation of eternal life. In the old scholastic language man's natural end depends upon his supernatural end.

This sense of the interpenetration of the natural and the supernatural, of the present life as the anticipation of eternal life, is shown by Traherne to derive from the centrality of love:

> Love is the true means by which the world is enjoyed: Our love to others, and others' love to us. We ought therefore above all things to get acquainted with the nature of Love. For Love is the root and foundation of nature: Love is the Soul of Life and Crown of rewards. If we cannot be satisfied in the nature of Love we can never be satisfied at all. The very end for which God made the world was that he might manifest His Love. Unless therefore we can be satisfied with his Love so manifested, we can never be satisfied. There are many glorious excellencies in the material world, but without Love they are all abortive. . . . Love in the fountain and love in the end is the glory of the world and the Soul of joy. Which it infinitely preferreth above all worlds, and delighteth in, and loveth to contemplate, more than all visible beings that are possible. So that you must be sure to see causes wherefore infinitely to be delighted with the love of God, if ever you would be happy.[20]

[19] In *Duty and Discernment,* ed. G. R. Dunstan, S.C.M. (1975), p. 14.
[20] *Centuries of Meditations,* Second Century, 62.

11

Conclusion

I have tried in this book to relate morality to certain pervasive features of the human condition, in terms of which its nature and purpose can be understood. I have not claimed that there can be no morality without religion, but I have suggested that much of the Western ethical tradition ultimately makes sense only if a religious view of the world is presupposed. Arguments of this sort are rarely coercive; and it remains open to the secular moralist to contend that a secular world-view of some kind can provide a rationale for the traditional conscience, or that Christianity cannot. I would hope to persuade him only that there is a serious case to be met. It is an important part of this case that, once the limits of a platitudinous morality have been passed, religious and other world-views inevitably affect people's judgements about the scope, character, and content of morality. They may not be aware of this and may be content to rely on their moral intuitions alone, without raising questions of justification, but our's is an age, like that of classical Greece, in which it is increasingly difficult to do so.

I am aware that in developing and illustrating this theme I have made assumptions and raised problems about which a great deal more needs to be said. That a philosophical thesis should be unproblematical is more than can reasonably be expected. Indeed there would be ground for suspicion if it were. The most that can be hoped is that the problems should be worth investigating further. Among the problems that manifestly arise are two in particular. The first is entirely general and concerns the relationship between world-views and moral intuitions. I have been concerned to argue that morality is affected by world-views, but also that it has an integrity of its own, so that one may properly reject a world-view if its moral implications are unacceptable. Morality does not have the sole word, but it does have a decisive word. The usual arguments for autonomy, of an intuitionist or Kantian kind, accord morality a greater degree of independence than, on my view, it possesses. Intuitions need checking and Kantian moral arguments hold only given certain assumptions. But, if this is so, is there any point at which moral considerations can be relied upon in criticism of a world-view? Should we not, to put it crudely, first look for a satisfactory world-view and then read off its moral implications, regardless of whether it satisfies our intuitions? There seems to be no middle way between regarding moral intuitions as entirely self-authenticating and allowing them no independent weight at all.

Part of the solution to this problem lies in recognizing that moral intuition is not an isolated faculty in the way that intuitionists have generally taken it to be. Moral judgements require to be supported by reasons, and the reasons are characteristically related to human needs. To be morally perceptive is to be aware implicitly of needs that are not immediately obvious and this requires gifts of sympathy and imagination which enable one to be more precisely aware of the true situation. When, for example, Hampshire complains of a 'coarseness and grossness of moral feeling, a blunting of sensibility'[1] as typical of utilitarian thinking, it is not only a moral lack that he remarks but a failure to notice significant facts about persons with which the moral defectiveness is associated. The psychological insight and the moral discernment are not identical, but the former is implicit in the latter. Strength and delicacy of moral feeling is an appropriate response to the needs of persons as sensitively recognized and justly assessed. The facts about persons that are relevant include some that are of deep structural importance, such as the continuity of persons over time. Failure to take adequate account of this continuity is, arguably, one of the reasons for a certain shallowness of thinking in utilitarian ethics and in some varieties of subjectivism. So there is in moral intuitions a tacit awareness of much that goes beyond the limits of the strictly moral and that requires to be taken into consideration when world-views are under discussion. It is possible, of course, to argue that we are not here dealing with facts, strictly so called, but with disputable theories about human personality or even, in some instances, with institutions that we are free to endorse

[1] Quoted on p. 72 above.

or not, as we choose.[2] But it is remarkable how much of the 'experience' that we appeal to in testing philosophies of life is of just this kind. And it is doubtful how far we can hope to arrive at facts which are entirely uninterpreted.

If an account along these lines of the relationship between moral discernment and awareness of facts about human nature (or, as we often put it, our 'experience of human nature') is correct, then it is evident that our moral intuitions cannot be discounted in any assessment of rival world-views. When B. F. Skinner in *Beyond Freedom and Dignity* develops a philosophy of life according to which many of our most characteristically human responses are held to be irrational, with ethical consequences that are reflected in his title, we are not being unreasonable if we reject it on that very ground. It is not just that we dislike the moral implications, but that to accept the underlying account of human nature would require us to jettison too much of the entire conceptual scheme with which we need to operate in understanding and dealing with one another. Whether in this particular instance we can go further and claim not only that it is unreasonable to accept Skinner's brand of naturalism, but also that we must reject it as logically incoherent, is a matter of acute philosophical controversy.[3] But, if our capacity for moral thinking is called into question by reducing mental processes to a complicated pattern of stimulus and response, it is at least arguable that the same is true of every kind of rational assessment, including that which is involved in the development and defence of Skinner's own theory.

We cannot, therefore, argue straightforwardly *either*: 'Here is an accredited world-view and these are its ethical implications; hence we must accept the latter without further ado'; *or*: 'This is morally inadmissible; therefore any world-view which permits it is to be rejected.' We must look for an overall position that will do justice to both moral and other considerations. Further reflection and experience may always in principle require us to modify our philosophy of life or revise

[2] Thus Mackie suggests that personal identity functions as an institution, and that institutions require endorsement, which we are free to withhold. See *Ethics*, p. 78, and also p. 71.

[3] See J. R. Lucas, *The Freedom of the Will*, Clarendon Press (1970), especially § 21.

our moral intuitions. Our predicament is complicated in practice by the fact that individuals (and even historical periods) vary in their capacity to appreciate and assess the different elements that go to make up a total philosophy of life, and, in the extent to which they are able to maintain a synoptic vision at all. We (that is to say 'we products of Western culture') have so strong a sense of the value of the individual, for example, that it strikes us as more indubitable than any metaphysical construction; it is easy, therefore, to suppose it quite unrelated to any, and to assume that our own vision must be shared by any reasonable man. But we know from other developed societies like classical Greece in Dover's study, [4] that this is not so. We have learned to see men in a certain way.

It is natural, and up to a point correct, to say that in so doing, we are simply reflecting a Christian view of man. Yet it is also somewhat misleading, because it suggests that what we find in people is not 'really' there but is contributed entirely by an interpretative scheme which comes, so to speak, entirely from outside. But when Helen Gardner[5] discovers in Shakespeare an essentially Christian sensibility she does not deny him a profound insight into human nature. Indeed Shakespeare is pre-eminently one of those who, to use Bayley's terms,[6] write about 'Nature' rather than about 'the Human Condition'. From the objectivist standpoint that I have been adopting we must rather say that Shakespeare's Christian sensibility enables him to see more truly into the realities of the human predicament. If this is so, our understanding of human nature and our moral discernment, which is inextricably bound up with it, must be allowed a large measure of genuine independence, enough to justify us in relying upon them to a very considerable extent in assessing, interpreting, modifying, and even rejecting a world-view.

This is one reason why it would be a mistake to conclude from the argument of this book that religious people are necessarily, or even as a rule, morally better or more sensitive than non-religious people; or that, in disputes between the Church and her critics, the Church must always have been

[4] See above, pp. 122–3.
[5] See above, p. 71.
[6] See above, pp. 82–3.

right. Specifically religious gifts, even when of a high order, are not invariably accompanied by equal moral sensitivity; and people of profound moral insight need not be religious. Shakespeare himself is not a religious poet, as Donne and Milton are.

Nevertheless, when due weight has been given to this consideration, there does seem reason to believe that, in a culture at large over an appreciable period of time, a moral tradition becomes ossified or disintegrates as it increasingly becomes divorced from the world-view which provides its ultimate rationale. This is why the Victorian Age, although preserving much that we are in process of losing, cannot be cited as a paradigm of Christian morality. The Victorians idolized morality, giving it that supreme importance which they were increasingly unable to accord to God.[7] Hence the morality they believed in and practised was in constant danger of becoming legalistic and joyless.

If it is correct that the search for a metaphysic of morals involves looking for a world-view that is both rationally defensible and in accord with moral intuitions that have been subjected to criticism and tested in experience, the alleged circularity of the Christian scheme can be seen not to be vicious. To the critic who complains that the entire scheme puts a question-begging reliance upon certain moral values, which it then purports to justify, e.g., upon love as a virtue and gratitude as a duty, we can reply that neither is required simply and solely by divine fiat. Given the nature of human beings as God created them, the obligation to show gratitude is a platitudinous one; and love in the sense of *agape*, although not platitudinous, is yet found in experience to answer a fundamental human need. In order to explain how and why this is so, we need, so the argument runs, to develop some understanding of divine love as it bears upon our human condition, above all as it is shown in the life and death of Christ, but we are so made as to be receptive to such understanding. Nature is such that it can be perfected by grace. Without God as the keystone the arch is incomplete and always liable to fall apart, but the keystone finds a space shaped to receive it.

[7] Cf. Gertrude Himmelfarb, *Victorian Minds*, Weidenfeld & Nicholson (1968), esp. chapter XI.

These remarks about nature and grace remind us that the entire argument has not only philosophical, but also theological implications. In trying to chart the theological frontier of ethics I have spent more time on the ethical than on the theological side, and the line I have taken fits some conceptions of theology better than others. Some contemporary Christian moralists may well complain that in undertaking a defence of the traditional conscience I have presupposed not only a broadly traditional ethic, but also an equally traditional theology. The argument does, indeed, imply that differences in theology will tend to issue in moral differences, and that, within theology, the same sort of dialectic is needed as between moral intuitions and world-views in general. There is, however, no possibility, as it seems to me, of a straightforward return to some conception of Christian ethics that has already been fully and satisfactorily formulated, associated with a theological system that has already been adequately worked out. Much work requires to be done if the Christian tradition, both in ethics and theology, is to be given appropriate expression in our contemporary situation. Nostalgia is not enough; although it is my impression that in our own day Christian moralists and theologians have often been too uncritical in their borrowings from the prevailing secular culture, taking over themes and attitudes which the more discerning secular thinkers have found increasingly untenable. This is one reason among many others why it is desirable that there should be more discussion than there has been in this century between Christian and secular thinkers, especially those of a liberal temper.

The comparative absence of such discussion has been due partly to a reluctance on the part of Christian theologians to adopt what they see as a 'triumphalist' position in relation to secular culture—to read off moral conclusions from theological premisses in a way that effectively denies the integrity of secular moral thought; partly to an assumption among intellectuals that no serious case can be made for theism. I have suggested that there is no generally agreed way of thinking about morality, and no generally agreed morality that is anything like complete. Beyond the platitudes there are divergences which derive from differing conceptions of what men need; and these in turn derive from differing conceptions of what men are. Christian theologians cannot, therefore, avoid being committed to certain distinctive moral notions, though there is warrant in Christianity itself for taking people's moral intuitions seriously, whether they are believers or not.

It is obvious that the argument of this book is no substitute for a reasoned case for theism and all along has had to assume that one is possible. It can, however, make some contribution to such a case; for, if our moral intuitions, together with the psychological and other insights they carry with them, can reasonably be trusted, and if they are more congruent with a Christian metaphysic than with any other, the latter is to some extent confirmed. Morality is one point of entry, and for many people a most important one, into a theistic world-view.

Nevertheless, it may be said, in the cultural circumstances of today, the most likely effect of any attempt to show a connection between religious belief and certain ways of looking at morality, is not to reinforce religious belief, or even to reawaken interest in it, but to loosen still further the hold of the traditional conscience. To the extent that the thesis is accepted, the secular thinker whose moral intuitions are still predominantly traditional will think it more reasonable to modify his conscience than to revise his opinions about Christianity.

Whatever may be thought about the general desirability of suppressing arguments whose acceptance, or even discussion, may have undesirable social consequences there is little case for doing so in the present instance. The moral confusion consequent upon the breakdown of a traditional culture is already with us and has been for several generations. As its effects become steadily more apparent, reflective individuals are increasingly aware of the need to 'choose between worlds', and are less and less likely to rest in inherited moral customs and attitudes through simple inertia. If they continue to hold on to them, it will be not through inertia but by a conscious act of faith, while they cast around for a view of life that can adequately sustain them. And, where so much is uncertain, it will be reasonable for them to do so. From a Christian point point of view they will be exhibiting what Simone Weil called

called 'a form of the implicit love of God',[8] and there is scriptural warrant for valuing this more highly than theological profession. What matters is that the alternatives should be clearly and sympathetically presented, and that Christianity itself should be articulated and, more importantly, shown in such a way as to be a genuine option. Whether, in the long term, as the issues become clearer, there will be a movement predominantly towards Christian belief or away from our traditional ethic on the part of such reflective minds it is impossible to forecast. But Christianity has, throughout its history, displayed a regenerative power that justifies not only faith but hope.

[8] 'Forms of the Implicit Love of God' in *Waiting on God*, tr. Emma Crawford, Routledge & Kegan Paul (1951).

Index